10 MINUTE
Clutter Control

10 MINUTE Clutter Control

Easy Feng Shui Tips for Getting Organized

SKYE ALEXANDER

METRO BOOKS
NEW YORK

This 2007 edition published by Metro Books,
by arrangement with
Fair Winds Press, a member of
Quayside Publishing Group,
100 Cummings Center
Suite 406-L
Beverly, MA 01915

Cover design by Laura Shaw Design
Cover illustration by Elizabeth Cornaro

Metro Books
122 Fifth Avenue
New York, NY 10011

ISBN-13: 978-07607-8937-7
ISBN-10: 0-7607-8937-1

Library of Congress Cataloging-in-Publication Data
Alexander, Skye.
    10-minute clutter control : easy feng shui tips for getting organized / Skye Alexander.
        p. cm.
Includes bibliographical references.
    ISBN 1-59233-068-1
    1. House cleaning. I. Title.
    TX324.A44 2004
    648'.5—dc22

                                                                2003022330

Printed and bound in United States

10 9 8 7 6 5 4 3 2

To my neat and orderly sister, Myke,
with gratitude for her constant encouragement.

Contents

INTRODUCTION

When I first started using feng shui (pronounced *fung SHWAY*) back in the mid-1980s, few people in the West had heard of it. Today, feng shui is a popular topic for magazine articles, radio programs, and TV talk shows. Scores of books have been written on the subject. You can buy feng shui candles, feng shui cosmetics, feng shui refrigerator magnets, feng shui greeting cards, and a host of other products that may or may not have any real value or any genuine relationship to this ancient Chinese art.

Yet there's still a lot of confusion about feng shui. Which of the many schools of thought is best? Why do even the experts disagree? Do you have to completely redo your home according to feng shui principles, or can you benefit from making just a few updates?

In my opinion, no particular school is better or worse, although some are easier and more convenient for Westerners to follow. Like experts in medicine, religion, golf, or any other field, feng shui practitioners subscribe to different theories and come to different understandings over time as a result of their own experiences. One thing just about everyone agrees on, however, is that clutter must be controlled. If you implement only one feng shui cure, get rid of the dirt, debris, and damage in your home.

10-Minute Clutter Control expands on some of the ideas I presented in my book *10-Minute Feng Shui*. It looks at the deeper significance of clutter in our homes and workplaces, how this affects us, and how we can remove obstacles in our lives simply by cleaning up the clutter around us.

How to Use This Book

10-Minute Clutter Control focuses on one essential feng shui cure—getting rid of clutter. Cures, by the way, are techniques designed to produce certain effects or to eliminate unwanted ones. In Chapter One, I explain the ABCs of feng shui and why it works. Chapters Two and Three discuss the symbolism and psychology of clutter and how you can eliminate problems in your life by eliminating clutter in your environment.

Chapters Four through Eight contain tips and solutions for clearing away clutter. These tips are grouped into five categories: home, workplace, areas outside your home, kids, and your personal life. Many can be implemented in ten minutes or so. The other, larger tasks, such as cleaning out an attic or basement, can be broken down into small segments to make them more manageable.

If you don't want to know much about feng shui, you can go directly to Chapter Four and get started. But if you're the sort of person who likes to understand *why* as well as *how*, the earlier chapters explain why making changes in your living and work areas will change your life.

The most important factor in successfully using feng shui is your intent—the physical cures are only part of the process. You'll get better results if you truly want to correct a particular problem and if you believe that what you are doing will work. In this sense, feng shui is a lot like other endeavors—the more you put into it, the more you get back.

CHAPTER ONE

How Feng Shui Works

Western society tends to think of luck as pure chance. The Chinese, however, believe we can cultivate and manipulate luck. Rather than simply playing the hand Fate dealt them in the game of life, they use an ancient practice called feng shui to remedy their problems and attract health, wealth, and happiness.

Feng shui's objective is to create harmony and balance in your environment. To accomplish this, feng shui masters apply a variety of practical solutions, called *cures*, to everyday problems. These remedies include such things as establishing convenient traffic patterns through your home, positioning furniture in comfortable arrangements, and eliminating clutter in your living and work spaces. There's nothing magical about these cures—they are sensible ways to make life easier and more efficient.

But feng shui also has a mystical component based on the *I Ching*, ancient Chinese philosophy, color and number symbolism, and other esoteric knowledge. Many of the cures feng shui recommends are symbolic as well as practical. The logical solutions enable you to function more effectively and comfortably; the symbolic ones influence your subconscious to change old patterns and conditioned responses that may be blocking you at a deeper level.

The Art of Placement

Feng shui is also known as the art of placement. By placing furniture, accessories, artwork, architectural elements, personal objects, and so on in particular spots, you create either a comfortable environment that people enjoy spending time in or an unpleasant one they can't wait to leave. Many good interior designers and architects unconsciously understand the principles of feng shui and use them automatically to create harmonious, well-balanced environments.

Even if you've never studied feng shui or interior design, you've undoubtedly experienced the effects of good and bad placement. For instance, if the first thing you encountered upon entering a living room was the back of a sofa, how would you feel? Unwelcome? Blocked? If you walked into an office and saw clutter everywhere, what would you think? That the person who worked there was so busy or distracted that he or she might not be able to pay attention to you? Once you start noticing your feelings and responses when you enter a space, you'll begin to understand how feng shui works.

Ch'i: Feng Shui's Pulse of Life

Literally translated, *feng shui* means *wind* and *water*. Wind and water, as we know, can be harnessed to produce energy. Feng shui also allows us to control and direct natural forces and utilize their energy constructively.

The principal force feng shui considers is ch'i (pronounced *chee*), the life-giving energy of the Universe that flows through everything—our homes, the Earth, our bodies. Acupuncturists use needles to eliminate blockages so ch'i can move freely in the body. Feng shui practitioners employ various cures, such as those discussed in Chapters Four through Eight, to keep ch'i flowing smoothly through our environments. One of the most common impediments to ch'i in our homes and workplaces is clutter. Clearing clutter from your environment is like unclogging a pipe so water can run through it again.

Ch'i travels through an area in much the same way you do. As you walk about your home, notice whether the pathways you normally use are easy to navigate or obstructed. Do they invite you to enter? Is it difficult to move through the space or to open windows and doors? Do some areas feel pleasant, others awkward or uncomfortable? You can't see ch'i, but after you work with it a while, you'll begin to sense its presence.

Ideally, you want ch'i to move through a space like a gently flowing stream or a light breeze. If it rushes by too quickly, it won't have time to bestow its life-giving benefits. If it gets "stuck" and sits like a stagnant pool, you may feel uneasy or even become physically ill. Clutter, debris, dirt, and disrepair interfere with the healthy flow of ch'i, producing tension, confusion, stuffiness, congestion, and a general feeling of malaise. Once clutter has been cleared away, other feng shui cures, such as lights, plants, sound, color, and mirrors, can be employed to rectify ch'i imbalances and create harmonious environments in which to live and work.

As Within, So Without

Our homes clearly demonstrate this axiom—so clearly that a feng shui master can walk through your home and see at a glance what's going on in your career, your family, your love life. From the point of view of feng shui, your home says a great deal about you—not only about your taste, but also which areas of your life are stable and balanced and which ones are incomplete, obstructed, or unsettled.

That's because your home is a symbol of you—the outer representation of your inner state. This powerful symbol not only reveals what's taking place in every area of your life, it also shows your attitudes toward your situation. How you furnish, decorate, clean, and arrange your living space express in graphic terms what's going on inside you—whether or not you are aware of it.

Here's an example. A woman I used to know was very private and refused to let many people get close to her. Her home, although large and well appointed, was so cluttered that there was no place to sit—a clear reflection of her reluctance to welcome visitors.

Take a good look at your own living space. If you're like most people, you'll notice that some areas are neat, clean, and orderly, while others are messy or neglected. Are your social areas inviting but your study chaotic? A feng shui practitioner might interpret this as an indication that you enjoy friendship and entertaining, but find work less appealing. Perhaps you've been meaning to organize or do repairs in a certain sector of your home, but never seem to get around to it. These disorderly parts correspond to unresolved issues in your life that you don't want to confront.

In Chapter Three, I'll show you how to analyze your home to spot problems. Then, in Chapter Four, I'll explain how you can fix your life by fixing your home.

Intention

The physical parts of feng shui can't be separated from the psychological ones. When you implement a cure—such as repositioning furniture, installing adequate lighting, or cleaning up clutter—you show that you want to improve conditions in your life by improving the condition of your environment. Once you decide you are ready for a change, you'll just naturally start applying feng shui cures in your home and workplace.

Your intention to take charge of your life and create your own luck is the most important part of feng shui. In a sense, your willpower is the active ingredient in feng shui, the power that makes it work.

Although feng shui cures will have an impact even if your heart isn't in it, you'll get better results if you are purposeful in what you do. If you lack sincerity or perform the cures without really intending to change your life, you may lapse back into old habits—such as allowing clutter to pile up again—and nullify the positive benefits of the cures you applied.

CHAPTER TWO

Is Clutter Controlling You?

Albert Einstein may not have known anything about feng shui, but his opinions on clutter control suggest he understood its basic concepts when he said, "Out of clutter, find simplicity. From discord, find harmony. In the middle of difficulty, lies opportunity."

Much of feng shui involves symbolic associations. Physical conditions in our environments symbolize emotional issues and attitudes we hold. Broken furniture, for instance, can signify broken dreams, physical injuries, or a breakdown in communication among family members. Dirty windows make it difficult to see situations clearly. Doors or drawers that stick may represent aspects of your life that are stuck.

It's easy to see the connection between physical clutter and messiness in your personal life. We even use the term "baggage" to describe old concepts, hang-ups, and behaviors that limit personal growth and happiness. If an area in your home is cluttered, you are probably experiencing confusion or blockages in the part of your life that corresponds to the cluttered section. Conversely, areas that you just naturally tend to keep neat and organized show the parts of your life that function smoothly. (I'll talk more about this in the next chapter.)

I have a friend whose home is extremely neat—except the area that's linked with love and relationships. This room is full of empty bottles and boxes, old paint cans, cast-off furniture, and cartons of memorabilia from his youth (including photo albums containing pictures of old girlfriends). The room has no heat and the roof leaks. No one who understands feng shui would be surprised to learn that this man has a lot of unresolved issues and outdated attitudes about women, love, and relationships.

Large-scale clutter produces physical obstacles that indicate the presence of psychological obstacles. The home of a man I know is so cluttered that his main rooms have been reduced to a few narrow pathways. Books and magazines, clothing, videos, dishes, electrical equipment, athletic gear, and more are stacked on top of furniture, forming shoulder-high barricades. This very fearful and withdrawn individual has unconsciously built a "clutter fortress" to hide behind.

Many people who lived through the Great Depression hoard stuff because they fear the poverty and shortages they experienced in their youth. When my father died in 1991, he still had K rations that he'd saved from World War II stashed in his kitchen closet. Holding on to old stuff, however, can keep you from letting go of the past and moving ahead with your life.

From the perspective of feng shui, clutter can represent several things:

- Confusion: Disarray and disorganization in your environment show that some areas of your life are messy or unsettled.

- Old baggage: Saving old, worn-out, unused items suggests that you are holding on to old ideas, attitudes, grudges, fears, or habits and allowing them to clutter your psyche.

- Obstacles: Piles of stuff represent blocks that limit your progress; they physically hamper your movement and hinder the flow of ch'i through your environment.

By clearing away the physical clutter around you, you can actually clear up disorder and difficulties in your life—sometimes overnight!

Clutter, Dirt, and Disrepair

From the perspective of feng shui, it's advantageous to free your home of clutter, dirt, and disrepair. Some homes are plagued by all three bugaboos, while others may suffer from only one. That's because each of these problems symbolizes something different.

Clutter refers to an accumulation of too much stuff, without proper organization or distinction. Clutter usually signifies confusion, lack of focus, chaos, instability, or muddled circumstances. If your home is cluttered, you may have too much going on and lack direction or a sense of priorities. Perhaps you are scattering your energy, rather than dedicating yourself to what's really important. You may be uncertain about your goals, who you are, or what you want in life. Often we see this sort of clutter in teenagers' rooms because they haven't sorted out these personal matters yet.

Dirt suggests low self-esteem, a low energy level, or poor health. Animals often stop cleaning themselves when they are sick or under stress. The same thing happens with people. If you lack vitality or enthusiasm for life, you may not see the value in cleaning your home. If your sense of self-worth is poor, you may not feel you deserve to live in pleasant surroundings.

Do you know people who always apologize for the unsightly condition of their home? These people are actually apologizing for the inadequacies they see in themselves.

Disrepair equates with despair. Broken furniture, cracked tiles, and crumbling plaster suggest broken dreams or a sense of hopelessness—your life seems to be falling down around you. Doors and windows that stick indicate feelings of being stuck or trapped by circumstances. Systems that don't work properly may symbolize self-imposed limits or areas in your life that aren't functioning adequately.

New Clutter, Old Clutter

In my home, clutter tends to collect in my office. As a freelance writer and artist, I'm often working on a number of projects simultaneously, and my desk may hold several stacks of paperwork that pertain to various jobs in progress.

"New clutter" of this sort usually indicates that you may be trying to do too much, that you lack focus and direction, or that you are letting things distract you from your primary path or purpose. New clutter can also include piles of CDs, clothing lying around, toys or sporting equipment scattered about—things you've used recently, but haven't bothered to put away. Cleaning up this clutter can help you to become more centered, focused, and effective.

"Old clutter" is all that outdated, unused stuff that tends to get stashed in the basement, attic, closets, and garage. Old paperwork in your files and old documents in your computer fall into this category, too. Lots of old clutter suggests you fear letting go of things that no longer have purpose in your life, even though they may actually be holding you back. Perhaps you are living in the past, are letting old ideas or emotions govern your present behavior, or are too security-conscious.

I used to work with a woman who never threw out any of the paperwork from her old jobs. Her files were stuffed with old folders, plans, cost sheets, etc. Although she rationalized that she might need to refer to this information someday, in reality she rarely did. With so much old clutter filling her drawers, the message she projected was that she didn't have room for new jobs, and so she subconsciously undermined her success. Once she realized the connection, she tossed most of her old paper-work and quickly attracted new business.

Workplace Clutter

Do you use a vertical filing system in your office? Do stacks of magazines, books, and file folders fill your work space? Do you have to shuffle through piles of paperwork to find something?

Disorganization in your work space wastes valuable time and money every day. How much does it cost you to search for mis-placed or inaccessible materials, return phone calls because you can't put your finger on information when you need it, redo work, replace supplies that you stashed someplace but can't remember where, and so on? A carpenter I know has so much clutter in his truck and workshop that often he can't find a tool he needs and has to buy a duplicate. In some work environ-ments, clutter can even lead to accidents and injury.

But clutter in your office has another drawback, too. It pre-vents you from focusing completely on the task at hand—your subconscious keeps reminding you of the unfinished business all around you. Over time, this can cause you to feel ineffective, unproductive, and overwhelmed. In her book *Taming the Paper Tiger*, Barbara Hemphill points out that "A cluttered desk indicates a pattern of postponed decisions."

Activity Clutter

Multitasking has become a way of life in our modern world. We pride ourselves on being able to juggle a number of operations simultaneously. We read the paper, talk to our loved ones, watch TV, go over our to-do lists, and eat breakfast all at the same time. At work, we follow the same pattern—scrolling through our e-mail while talking on the phone, filing paperwork, and jotting down appointments on our calendars. Even when we're engaged in a single activity—particularly a mindless one like unloading the dishwasher or raking leaves—we're usually thinking about something other than the task at hand. Yet no matter how busy we are, we rarely feel a sense of accomplishment at the end of the day—most likely because we haven't truly experienced anything we've done.

When you try to do several things at once, you can't pay attention to—or enjoy—any of them fully. Confusion, stress, and forgetfulness are the inevitable results of this "activity clutter." How often have you laid down something when you were involved in some other activity and forgotten where you left it? How many times do you have to ask someone to repeat what he or she just said because you were thinking about something else?

In his book *Timeshifting*, Stephan Rechtschaffen, M.D., suggests that we should learn to focus our attention and live in the moment. Doing so reduces the confusion and stress produced by activity clutter. His Holiness the Dalai Lama even recommends against talking while you are eating, because in order to get the full benefit of either activity you must focus on it completely. When our attention is fragmented, we feel disconnected and derive less satisfaction from what we're doing. We end up missing out on what's going on right now—which is most of life!

Activity clutter also includes packing our days and nights with so many engagements, projects, and tasks that we rarely have a free moment to just be. One of the reasons we fill our lives with busyness is so we won't have to confront our feelings—and ourselves. To avoid looking deeply at ourselves, we surf the Internet, watch television, talk on the phone, do household chores, work out, go shopping.

Some of us load ourselves up with activities in order to boost our sense of importance. When many demands are placed on us, we feel needed. We don't delegate responsibilities to others because we like to think we're the only ones who can handle the job. If we're constantly doing something, we feel like we're making progress, even if we're really just spinning our wheels.

Controlling activity clutter requires you to examine your life and assign value to the various activities in which you engage. It may help to write down on a piece of paper all the activities you participate in on a weekly basis. List these activities under headings such as *Essential* (eating, going to work, doing laundry, etc.), *Enjoyable* (going to lunch with friends, playing the piano, reading bedtime stories to the children), *Optional* (shopping, watching TV, surfing the Internet), and *Obligatory* (serving on a committee you wish you hadn't volunteered for, catering to an elderly relative's whims).

Examine your list with a critical eye, with the goal of reducing activity clutter by, say, 20 percent. Ask yourself some pointed questions: Are you devoting entirely too much time to some of the things on your list or doing them to avoid another part of life? For example, do you really need to watch every televised basketball game, pro and college? Are you letting someone else dictate how you spend your time or shouldering more than your fair share? Can you cut back on some of these duties, entrust them to someone else, or eliminate them entirely? What would happen if you did?

Relationship Clutter

Most of us know people we'd rather not spend time with, yet out of a sense of duty or guilt or good manners, we allow ourselves to be drawn into unwanted associations. Some of these people simply waste our time or distract us from more important things in our lives. Others actually drain our energy or have a negative influence on us.

There's no law that says you have to give time and energy to people you don't like or who aren't good for you. You don't have to be rude, but be clear and honest with these people. Depending on the circumstances, let them know you'd prefer not to spend as much time with them as you have in the past or that you don't wish to continue your association with them at all.

Even people we care about can clutter our lives with their problems, needs, and expectations. Family members, in particular, may not understand or respect the importance of personal boundaries. Friends may enjoy your company and want to include you in all their activities or share everything that's going on in their lives with you. If your friends or loved ones are cluttering your emotional space so that you feel you don't have enough time or energy for other things you want to do, set limits—for yourself and them. Learn to say no and stick to it. Explain, nicely, that you have work to do, need some time to yourself, are being drawn off-center—whatever the case may be. In relationships with other people, quality is more important than quantity.

Relationship clutter has another aspect, too. The *I Ching*, or *Book of Changes*, to which feng shui is closely connected, is not just an oracle, it's a three-thousand-year-old guide to living in harmony with the Universe. Much of the advice the *I Ching* offers involves relating to other people. Following its wisdom can help us eliminate clutter—confusion, tension, conflict, and other difficulties—in our personal relationships.

According to the *I Ching*, we clutter our relationships when we place too many of our own expectations on other people— when we expect them to fulfill our desires or satisfy our demands. A father who expects his son to be the star athlete he always wanted to be in his own youth, for example, adds clutter to the son's life. The need for ego gratification can also produce relationship clutter. If, for instance, we constantly look to other people to validate us or to boost our egos, we make unreasonable demands on them and may take offense if they don't give us the attention we want. In Chapter Eight, I include some tips for reducing this sort of relationship clutter.

Mental Clutter

Although the term *senior moment* has entered our vocabulary as a synonym for forgetfulness, memory gaps are more often due to inattention and "mental clutter" than to actual disease or intellectual decline. The truth is, most of us, regardless of age, lack mental focus and clarity. We've become an attention deficit disorder society.

To see just how cluttered your mind is, set a timer for one minute. Try to hold a single thought for that brief span of time—it's harder than you might imagine. How many other thoughts popped into your head?

Mental clutter keeps us from being as productive as we could be. We derail our trains of thought thousands of times a day. Each time we allow ourselves to become sidetracked, we lose momentum.

Television is one of the most common and insidious sources of mental clutter. The omnipresent TV constantly bombards us with pictures and noise. We channel surf, glimpsing disconnected bits and pieces, without processing what we've seen. Many of us leave the set turned on as background noise, where it continues to clutter the subconscious mind. Much of what we see and hear on TV is not just useless information, it's damaging to our mental clarity and peace of mind. Your mind retains everything it witnesses and stores it someplace in your brain, even if you aren't aware that this is happening. Do you really need to see the same news stories rebroadcast morning, noon, and night? Repeated viewing of scenes of war, murder, fires, accidents, and so on can be mentally and emotionally disconcerting. Surveys have shown that people who watch a lot of television believe the world is a more dangerous place than those who rarely view TV.

Meditation is one of the best ways to reduce mental clutter. Meditating for just ten minutes each day will improve your concentration and clarity, calm nervous tension and stress, and increase your sense of well-being. Some people who meditate regularly say it produces all sorts of other benefits, too, such as helping them to sleep better, enriching their creativity, diminishing worries and fears, and enhancing their relationships with others. Professional athletes have even improved their skills as a result of daily meditation.

Atmospheric Clutter

Have you ever walked into a room and felt bad vibes, even though you couldn't identify the cause? Buildings retain the energetic vibrations of their inhabitants for a long time—especially vibrations generated by strong emotions. The combined vibes produced by all the feelings, actions, sounds, and even thoughts of the people who have spent time in your home can add up to atmospheric clutter.

Therefore, it's a good idea to "clear the air" in your home periodically. Open the windows and allow fresh air to circulate through your space. *Smudging* is an easy and pleasant way to cleanse your environment of atmospheric clutter. White sage is one of the best materials for smudging, but incense—particularly pine, peppermint, eucalyptus, or sandalwood—will work fine, too. Light a bundle, cone, or stick of sage or incense and let its fragrant smoke waft through each room of your home.

Perform this purifying ritual to disperse unwanted vibrations before you move into a new place. You'll also want to cleanse your home after an argument or other distressing experience, after a party or large gathering, or if you sense that the space feels uncomfortable in any way. Furniture, jewelry, and other objects also retain the vibrations of previous owners, so before you use them, smudge antiques and preowned items to remove traces of other people's energy.

CHAPTER THREE

Clear Your Clutter, Clear Your Life

"All items produce sound, smell, color, texture, or shape and have various energies that can clutter and block optimum function. Having too many items can dilute the special energies of items that you love and that are purposeful in their placement," explains feng shui consultant Jami Lin. "The less clutter you have, the more your favorite items can be featured and radiate their life-enhancing energies."

This doesn't mean you should pare down your belongings until your home is as bare-bones as a Zen monastery. I have a friend who prides himself on his clutter-free existence. By rejecting possessions, however, he reveals his reluctance to place value on anything or to make commitments to people, community, and personal goals. The objects with which we surround ourselves—particularly those we prize most—say a lot about us. The point is to highlight your treasures—the things that give you joy to use, wear, or look at, regardless of their monetary worth—and eliminate those that have no particular significance. Getting rid of clutter is like weeding a garden so the flowers have room to thrive.

What to save and what to toss is an entirely personal matter. The renowned English designer and craftsman William Morris believed you should "have nothing in your houses that you do not know to be useful or believe to be beautiful." That's good advice to follow when you are trying to decide what stays and what goes. If you still can't make up your mind, box items you aren't ready to part with yet, label the boxes, and store them for a period of time, maybe six months to a year. At a later date, you can reconsider how important they are to you.

The Bagua

The Chinese believe that all life is interconnected, that our environments influence us and we influence our environments. To a feng shui master, your home presents a detailed and revealing picture of you—it shows which parts of your life are in good working order and which ones could use a little TLC.

Some popular types of feng shui employ an octagon-shaped tool called the *bagua* (pronounced *bah-kwah*) to determine which parts of your home correspond to which areas of your life. This device has links to the *I Ching*, but you don't need to plumb the depths of ancient Chinese wisdom to use the bagua. All you have to do is lay it over a sketch or floor plan of your home. (See diagram on following page.)

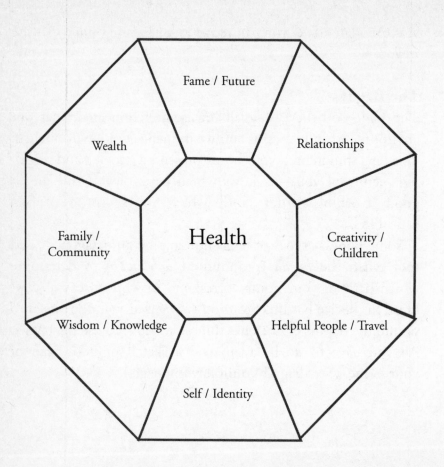

As you can see in this diagram, the bagua is divided into nine sectors, called *gua*, each one relating to a different facet of your life:

- Self/Identity: Your self-image, your sense of identity, your work or purpose in life

- Wisdom/Knowledge: Your attitudes toward knowledge, your spiritual path, how you learn and share information

- Family/Community: Your parents, extended family, heritage, neighbors, and community

- Wealth: Your finances; your ability to earn, attract, and hold on to money

- Fame/Future: Your public image, how you project yourself in the world, your career, future goals, and potential

- Relationships: Marriage or romantic partner, your attitudes toward love and relationships, interactions with a partner

- Creativity/Children: Children of the mind or body, self-expression, creative endeavors

- Helpful People/Travel: Friends, associates, support network (including doctors, attorney, accountant, mechanic, etc.), travel

- Health: Physical well-being or challenges

Using the Bagua

The entrance you use most often to go in and out of your home is the starting point for analyzing your living space with the bagua. This may be a side or back door, or even an entryway through a garage, rather than the front door. If you live in an apartment building, the door to your own apartment is more important to consider than the main entrance to the building.

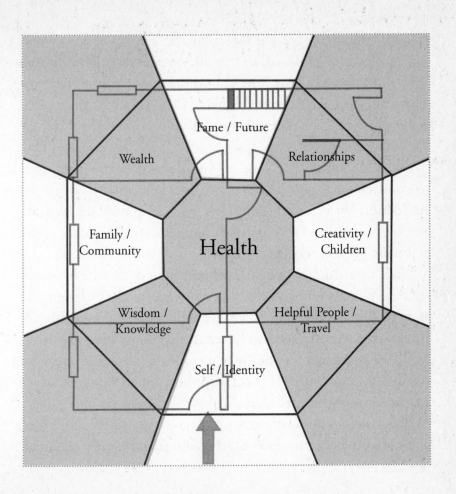

Align the arrow on the bagua at the center of the wall in which this door is placed, so that the octagon is super-imposed on your home's interior. You can do this in your mind's eye, or physically lay a bagua over a drawing of your home's floor plan. Your entrance will fall in the Self Gua, Wisdom Gua, or Helpful People Gua.

Some schools of feng shui say you should use the front door as your reference point, even if you generally enter through the back door, but I haven't found this practice to produce accurate results. You may want to try both methods and decide for yourself which one works best.

Now you can see which gua correspond to which rooms or areas of your home. Once you've identified the different gua in your home, you can quickly see which parts of your life are being adversely affected by clutter and set about clearing them.

Recently I visited the home of a couple of Texas artisans who wanted to know how they could improve their finances. Most of the time they entered and left their home via the garage. When I mentally positioned the bagua over their floor plan, their Wealth Gua turned out to be almost completely occupied by two very large closets that were jammed full of stuff. I suggested that they immediately start using their front door instead, which would rearrange the order of the gua in their home. I also recommended getting rid of some of the clutter in their closets in order to make room for new money-making possibilities to enter their life. A week after they started using their front door, the woman won $1,500 in a contest and the couple sold $5,000 worth of their artwork. The next week, the man (who is also a realtor) sold a half-million-dollar house he'd had listed for more than two years. You can bet they're believers now!

You can also analyze each room of your home using the bagua in the same way. Position the bagua so that the arrow lines up with the entrance to the room (or the wall in which this entrance is placed). The different gua will align with the various parts of the room. In this way, you can fine-tune your home and the related parts of your life.

For instance, you may notice that although your living room is generally pretty neat, the section that corresponds to neighbors is cluttered. This might show that even though your social life is relatively happy, you are experiencing some problems with your immediate neighbors. Clearing the clutter in this portion of the room can enable you to clarify the situation outside your home.

The bagua can also give you a bigger picture if you superimpose it over a plot plan of your yard (or, if you live in an apartment, over the entire building). Line up the arrow with the entrance to the property—your driveway, for instance, or the main entrance to an apartment building. The back left portion of your yard is the Wealth Gua, the back right section is the Relationships Gua, and so on. Like the interior of your home, your yard graphically describes what's going on in your life.

Shortly after I got divorced, a tree in my yard that had died during the previous year (while my marriage was deteriorating) fell down in a big storm. Interestingly, the tree was located just about where the Relationships Gua and the Creativity Gua intersect. The dead tree obviously symbolized the end of my marriage, but its collapse turned out to be a positive symbol: My former husband had not been very supportive of my creative endeavors, and when the dead tree toppled over, it indicated that the divorce had cleared the way for me to spend more time writing and painting.

As this example shows, the condition of your yard also impacts your life. Keeping your property clutter-free and well maintained has a positive effect on your health, wealth, and happiness. In Chapter Six, I offer a number of feng shui cures that you can do outside your home to increase the benefits you attract.

What Does Your Home Say About You?

If you're like most people, some areas of your home are more orderly than others—like my friend who only cluttered up his Relationships Gua. A cluttered Family Gua, for instance, suggests confusion, stress, or disharmony among family members. A messy Wealth Gua usually indicates that your finances are unsettled, chaotic, troublesome, or that you aren't comfortable handling money matters. A Wealth Gua that's jam-packed with stuff, like the one in the home of the Texas couple, shows that profitable opportunities are blocked and/or your income is stagnant.

A friend who admits to being the world's worst housekeeper has a particularly unsightly Wealth Gua in her home. This bright and talented woman is always struggling to make ends meet. She comes from a family that overemphasized wealth and used money as a tool for manipulation. Not surprisingly, she has some issues concerning money and is unconsciously undermining her financial success by cluttering up her home. Although she often talks about cleaning and organizing her messy house, she never seems to get around to it—and probably won't, until she decides to address her confusion over money, values, and self-worth.

In the process of clearing the clutter in your own environment, you may find that you encounter some emotional resistance. Even though you haven't worn that coat or used that waffle iron in years, you may be reluctant to let go of it. Ask yourself why you are holding on to something—the answers could be quite revealing.

What's so fascinating about feng shui is that once you recognize that you are creating your own life situations with your attitudes—and that these attitudes are mirrored in the physical condition of your home—you can rectify the problems. By controlling clutter, you can literally take control of your life.

As you begin clearing the clutter from the various gua, you'll notice changes starting to take place in your life. Often these changes occur over a period of time, but sometimes they happen almost immediately. The day my "significant other" started tearing down walls and ripping up carpet in the master bedroom of a house he'd purchased for our winter home in another part of the country, I began feeling agitated—even though I was two thousand miles away and thought the project wouldn't get under way until the following week. I felt disoriented and disrupted—just like the physical changes that were taking place in the master bedroom. Walls were coming down, new windows and doors and closets were going in, and so on. Now, I'm waiting to see how our relationship evolves as the renovation progresses—maybe we'll need to take down "walls" and put new "windows" and "doors" in our relationship.

You may be amazed at how even a few simple adjustments can affect your finances or love life. For this reason, you may not want to tackle everything at once. Instead, choose one gua—or a portion of a gua—and put that in order. Wait a while and see what changes come about before cleaning up another section.

Missing Gua

Unless your home is a perfect square, rectangle, circle, or octagon, you may be missing part of or a whole gua. Usually this means that a portion of your life is absent, problematic, or unimportant to you. Don't despair—feng shui provides cures for just about every irregularity, including missing gua.

If you are a homeowner and can physically remedy this deficiency, you may want to build a deck, patio, garden, or other addition to complete the missing sector. If that's not an option, you can fill in the gap with what's called a "symbolic corner." Using your imagination, extend the footprint of your home to a point where the missing walls would join. Place something here to mark the symbolic corner—a plant, light, flagpole, statue, birdbath, large stone, etc.

If you live in an apartment and can't make major changes in the building's structure, you can symbolically cut holes in the walls that chop up your living space and eliminate a gua. Simply hang mirrors on the walls that cut off the gua to symbolically expand your apartment beyond its physical limitations. Or, if you prefer, hang pictures of landscapes with distant views to create the illusion of space beyond the actual walls of your apartment.

Symbolic Associations

As we've already seen, much of feng shui relies on symbols and symbolic associations. In the process of uncluttering your home, consider the associations you attach to the things you choose to keep. Function, monetary worth, and sentimental value are only part of the picture. Even if an area is clutter-free, the symbolism of the articles you place there can have tremendous impact. Think about the meaning of a particular gua and whether the items you plan to put in it are compatible with the gua's significance—and your own intentions.

Here's a story that perfectly illustrates what I mean. A divorced woman I know wanted to find new love, but her relationships never seemed to go beyond an initial date or two.

Mirrors can be used inside to symbolically "cut through" obstructing walls.

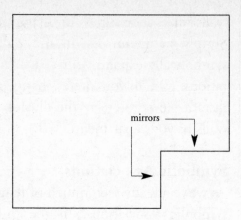

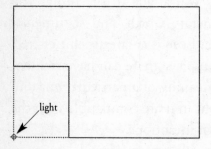

Lights used outside can "fill in" missing sectors of an L-shaped building. A tree could produce the same effect.

When I examined the Relationships Gua of her bedroom, I discovered the reason. On top of a chest of drawers in this section, she'd placed a jewelry box, and inside the box were pieces of jewelry her former husband had given her—including her old engagement and wedding rings! These items had monetary value and she didn't want to part with them, but the symbolic connections kept her bound to her ex and prevented her from attracting a new partner. Soon after she moved the jewelry to a safe-deposit box, the woman began a new relationship.

You can intentionally use symbols for specific purposes or to produce desired results. Coins, crowns, gems, champagne, and pictures of castles or Cadillacs, for instance, are symbols we associate with wealth. When placed in the Wealth Gua of your home or workplace, they encourage prosperity. We connect hearts, flowers, and doves with love, so these symbols can have a beneficial influence when placed in your Relationships Gua. Although some symbols mean pretty much the same thing to everyone, others are personal and may hold special significance for you alone. One spring, for example, a bird built a nest in a wreath I'd hung on my front door; soon three baby birds appeared. I took this as a positive indicator of creativity and new opportunities coming my way—and indeed, I soon received a contract to write a new book.

Shapes are simple symbols, too. Circles, for example, are universal symbols of wholeness and union. Arrows point in a certain direction and suggest movement. In feng shui, we can tap the deeper meanings inherent in shapes to create the circumstances we desire. Often, feng shui cures (including some of those in the following chapter) use shapes to produce effects. The following list briefly explains the meanings of some familiar geometric shapes.

Shapes and Their Meanings

Circle = wholeness, continuity, unity, harmony, heaven

Square = solidity, permanence, stability, earth

Triangle = movement, change, direction toward a goal

Rectangle = growth, expansion

Curved or wavy lines = flexibility, interaction, adaptability

Straight lines = rapid movement, single-mindedness, focus

Although we tend to think of numbers as tools for counting and quantifying, they also have symbolic associations. Two, for instance, represents partnership. As you go about reducing clutter in your living and work spaces, keep in mind the number of items you choose to leave or highlight in a certain gua and the significance attached to them. If you hope to attract a mate, you don't want to clear away all but one object in your Relationships Gua!

The Chinese consider the number three and its multiples—especially nine—to be lucky. The following list explains the feng shui symbolism generally connected with numbers.

1 = individuality, beginnings, focus

2 = partnership, polarity, balance

3 = expansion, creativity, action, opportunity

4 = stability, solidity, form

5 = change, movement, instability

6 = harmony, supportiveness, give-and-take

7 = introspection, solitude, wisdom

8 = permanence, business, money

9 = completion, fullness, good fortune

Even the materials used in your home or office furnishings have symbolic associations in feng shui. According to Chinese philosophy, the world is composed of five elements—fire, earth, water, wood, and metal. Each of these elements depicts a different aspect of ch'i and operates in its own unique way to produce a specific effect. Fire stimulates, earth stabilizes, water softens and blends, wood expands, metal strengthens and concentrates.

As you go about reducing clutter and creating order in your life, you'll want to take into account the elemental balance in your living and work environments to prevent "elemental clutter." Too much fire in a room can cause tension and instability; too much metal can result in rigidity. In much the same way that you might prepare a recipe, you can combine and adjust the elements in your home or workplace in any way you choose to bring about the conditions you desire. For example, add metal objects to children's bedrooms to help them concentrate and focus on their studies. Add wooden items to your office to encourage new business and financial growth.

You don't have to be a feng shui master to incorporate the five elements auspiciously in your home or workplace—the following table shows which everyday objects fall into which elemental category. (Some actually incorporate two elements— a brick fireplace, for instance, blends fire and earth.) Your goal is to combine the elements in your environment so that all are represented and no single element overwhelms the others.

The Five Elements

Fire: electricity, candles, fireplace, stove, lighting, computer, heating system, TV/stereo, clothes, dryer

Earth: brick, stone, ceramic tile, marble, china, rugs

Water: glass items, sink, toilet, tub, pool, plumbing, aquarium, washing machine, windows, dishwasher

Wood: wooden items, paper items, plants, linens, books, newspapers

Metal: metal items, pots and pans, silverware, refrigerator, hand tools

Clutter in the Workplace

Many of us spend almost as much time at work as we do at home. Therefore, it's important to use feng shui in your place of employment, too. In China, huge multinational companies as well as tiny noodle shops employ feng shui practitioners to help them optimize their business prospects.

The building in which a company is housed describes the condition of the business itself. Have you ever noticed how some locations never seem to be able to support a business for very long and the occupant turnover rate is quite rapid? From a feng shui perspective, it's usually easy to see why.

You can use the bagua to analyze your workplace, just as you did your home. Simply superimpose the octagon over a floor plan or diagram of the store, office building, factory, or wherever you work to see which gua relate to which sections of the operation.

The various gua describe situations similar to those they relate to in a home. The Helpful People Gua, for example, represents suppliers, distributors, colleagues, bankers, lawyers, advisors, etc.; the Relationships Gua symbolizes professional contacts and interactions between workers. Obviously, the Wealth Gua and Fame/Future Gua are very important, and careful attention should be paid to these areas. If your business uses a cash register or safe, put it in the Wealth Gua. If travel is a major part of your business, keep this area in top-notch condition.

Some years ago, I worked for a firm that was housed in a beautifully renovated schoolhouse. The offices were conveniently laid out, with high ceilings, lots of windows, and attractive color schemes. The lobby was handsomely furnished with antiques. However, a large, practically empty conference room occupied the Wealth Gua. The room was rarely used—in fact, one of its primary purposes seemed to be for storage of boxes of stuff that nobody knew what to do with. Shortly after I left the company, it ran into financial trouble, and before long most of the employees had been laid off. I often wonder what might have happened had that important section of the building been better utilized.

Workplace clutter can increase stress, interfere with clear communication, cause delays and mistakes, disrupt plans, and result in general confusion that can impair the prosperity, success, and well-being of all concerned. In some workplaces, such as restaurant kitchens and factories where potentially dangerous equipment is used, clutter can even lead to injuries.

In a work environment, clutter has a detrimental effect on each individual in the organization as well as on the overall company. Most of us have experienced problems associated with clutter in our workplaces. Perhaps you've wasted time hunting through stacks of file folders that weren't put away properly, or missed a meeting because the memo announcing it was at the bottom of your in-box, or covered up an important document with piles of paperwork. As companies cut back on their workforces to save money and employees are required to handle ever-increasing workloads, clutter-free environments become even more essential to the smooth operation of businesses. In Chapter Five, I offer some quick and easy tips for improving your work environment by clearing physical and atmospheric clutter.

CHAPTER FOUR

Control Clutter in Your Home

Make sure the entrance to your home is clear and accessible.

Visitors to your home get their first impressions of you from your entranceway. Make certain your front door, porch, steps, and other nearby areas are neat, so they speak well of you. Ch'i comes in through the doors of your home, too. A cluttered or obstructed entryway blocks this life-generating force and inhibits your health, wealth, and happiness.

Keep your foyer clear of clutter.
The foyer serves as a transition zone from the outside to the interior of your home. To make guests—and ch'i—feel welcome, this area should be neat, clear, and inviting. Obstacles in your foyer that make it difficult for visitors to move into the other parts of your home will also interfere with the amount of ch'i that can enter and energize your life.

Hang a wind chime in your entryway.
To prevent ch'i from getting stuck in your entryway, hang a wind chime from the ceiling. The chime symbolically circulates positive energy throughout your home. Its pleasing sound also breaks up atmospheric clutter that can collect in a small, windowless, or self-contained foyer, mudroom, or anteroom. Ring the chime upon entering to clear the air.

Clear the walkways through your home.
Keep the pathways through your home free of furniture, clutter, and other obstructions. Can you move comfortably from one room to the next? Can you easily access windows and closets? Or do you have to sidestep walls, furnishings, or piles of clutter? Obstacles in your home's passageways block the smooth flow of ch'i into the various gua and limit the benefits it brings.

Clean out a closet in your living room.
Closets symbolize the hidden parts of ourselves. When you clean out and neatly organize a closet, you demonstrate your willingness to remove old attitudes, habits, and behavior patterns that can cause confusion or blockages in your life. Because

the living room is the place where socializing often takes place, cleaning out a closet here can improve your social life. This cure also can have a positive effect on your public image and your interactions with other people in general.

~

Clean out a closet in your Wealth Gua.
If a closet in your Wealth Gua is jam-packed with stuff, you may be blocking new moneymaking opportunities. To make room for prosperity to enter your life, clean out a closet in your Wealth Gua. Getting rid of clutter here can also help you uncover hidden issues you may be harboring about money and what it represents to you.

~

Clean out a closet in your Relationships Gua.
Many of us have old attitudes, fears, and "baggage" that can cause problems in our romantic relationships. Just

closing the door on problems won't make them go away. By cleaning out a closet in your Relationships Gua, you demonstrate your willingness to address these issues. If your goal is to attract new love into your life, you'll increase your chances if you first let go of old stuff that keeps you stuck in the past. Getting rid of clutter can also improve an existing relationship by eliminating obstacles, resentments, rigidity, and confusion.

Keep closet doors shut.
Closets represent the private side of your life, because this is where you store things out of sight when you aren't using them. Even after you've uncluttered your closets, keep their doors shut to prevent personal matters from becoming public knowledge.

Dust lampshades.

Lamps symbolize the sun's life-giving energy and promote positive feelings. From the perspective of feng shui, light boosts your vitality, stimulates opportunity, and encourages growth. Keep lampshades clean to maximize the amount of light in your home.

> TIP: Be sure to turn on the lights periodically in rooms or areas that don't get used often—this keeps ch'i from stagnating in these spots.

Wash a mirror.

In feng shui, mirrors are very powerful cures because they visually "double" what they reflect. A dirty mirror obstructs and diminishes this power. Keep mirrors clean and sparkling—and pay attention to the views they reflect.

Neatly arrange objects in front of a mirror.
It's doubly important to neatly arrange the objects you place in front of a mirror. Because mirrors visually "double" what they reflect, they'll exacerbate confusion, chaos, problems, or upsets if they reflect clutter.

TIP: To further enhance the power of this cure, place the mirror and the object in the appropriate gua in your home—see Chapter Three for information about the different gua and their associations.

Place treasures in front of a mirror.
In front of a mirror, place objects that hold special meaning for you or that symbolize things you want to expand in

your life. The doubling power of the mirror will heighten the meaning of the object and double its influence. To increase your prosperity, for instance, set one of your personal treasures or an item that you associate with wealth where it will be reflected in a mirror.

~

Use the one-a-day clutter-clearing method.
If clearing away your clutter seems like an overwhelming task, take it a step at a time. Just get rid of one thing you don't need each day—throw it out, give it to someone else who'll enjoy it, recycle it, or donate it to charity.

~

Pack away off-season clothes as soon as you stop wearing them.
From a practical point of view, this uncluttering cure frees up closet and drawer space and makes it easier to find what you

want to wear. On a psychological level, it enables you to put the past behind you so you can move forward and embrace each new season of your life.

~

Get rid of clothing you no longer wear.
If you haven't worn something in a year, you probably don't need it. Unless a garment has special significance, it doesn't warrant space in your closet or dresser. Give it to a friend or charity—or take it to a consignment shop where your clutter can earn cash.

~

Eliminate duplicates.
How many white shirts, black skirts, or blue striped ties do you really need? Pare down your wardrobe by eliminating duplicate items. Keep the ones you like best and that look best on you— Take the rest to a consignment shop or donate them to charity.

Get rid of clothing that doesn't go with anything else.
Do you have garments that don't coordinate with anything else in your closet? Usually this means that either the color or style isn't really you. Pass them on to someone who'll appreciate them.

Don't hold on to clothes that are too big.
If you're on a diet, you may undermine your success by holding on to clothes that are a larger size than your target. Get rid of garments that represent the old image you are trying to shed. Knowing that you'll have to replace an entire wardrobe if you gain weight can be an added incentive to stick to your diet.

Choose a personal color palette and only buy clothing in that palette.

Most people look better in some colors than in others. Determine what your best colors are and only buy clothing in those hues. This allows you to reduce the number of garments in your closet while actually increasing your wardrobe's versatility, because everything goes with everything else. This cure also facilitates shopping—you can bypass everything that isn't in your personal color palette.

Reduce suitcase clutter.

Lay out on your bed all the clothing you plan to take with you on a trip. Put half of it back in your closet and pack what's left. If possible, try to fit everything you need for a short trip into a carry-on bag—you won't have to wait for your luggage when you arrive or risk losing it en route.

> TIP: Choosing clothing within a limited color range makes this easy and increases the versatility of the outfits you pack.

Don't iron clothing before packing it.
This saves time and effort, as garments tend to get crumpled in your suitcase regardless of how carefully you pack them. Wait until you get where you're going to iron clothes rather than doing it twice.

Label shoe boxes.
If you store your shoes in boxes to protect them, eliminate guesswork by labeling the boxes so you can see at a glance

what's inside. Clear, stackable plastic boxes with lids that allow you to see your shoes work great, too.

~

Organize shoes to reduce closet clutter.
Even if you don't have as many shoes as Imelda Marcos, they can still clutter up your closet. Group shoes according to season, color, style, and frequency of use. Keep shoes you wear regularly in the most convenient place. Store special-occasion shoes farther back. If space is limited, move off-season shoes out of your primary clothes closet. Here again, the "how many do you really need" rule applies—if you have six pairs of black heels, you can probably get rid of a couple of pairs.

~

Use plastic bags to stuff the toes of shoes.
Most of us have more plastic bags than we know what to do with. Instead of using expensive wooden shoehorns to keep

your shoes in shape, stuff the toes of your shoes with wadded-up plastic bags.

~

Get rid of broken jewelry and pieces you don't wear.
Gemstones retain energetic vibrations for a long time—that's why some psychics can "read" a person from her jewelry. Repair or get rid of broken jewelry, which can signify breaks in your relationships, your career path, or your finances. Either give pieces you don't wear to someone who will enjoy them or take them to a consignment shop.

~

Organize jewelry conveniently.
Bait and tackle boxes, like the ones fishermen use, are great for organizing jewelry. The small compartments keep earrings together and prevent necklaces from getting tangled.

Keep jewelry neat while traveling.

When you're traveling, use plastic organizers designed for pills and vitamins to keep earrings and other jewelry neat. Some mail-order vitamin companies offer these handy containers free with purchases.

TIP: When you aren't wearing them, fasten the clasps on necklaces to prevent tangles.

Stack plates and napkins together.
To keep china plates from being scratched or chipped, stack them with a folded cloth napkin between each plate. This not only prevents damage, it facilitates setting the table because you grab both plates and napkins at the same time.

Clear clutter from your dining room table.
If you don't use your dining room table very often, it may end up being a clutter collector. Clutter on your dining room table can produce tension or problems between members of your household—clear it away promptly.

Trim houseplants.
Plants symbolize growth—keep yours neatly trimmed to encourage new growth in your life. Dry, brown leaves are not only unattractive, they represent death, decay, and stagnant conditions. Spindly vines suggest things are growing out of control and need to be reined in.

Wash a plant's leaves.
Living plants are a favorite feng shui cure—place a plant in an area where you want to encourage growth (see Chapter Three for information about the different gua and their associations). To help plants grow and look better, wash dust off their leaves periodically so they can breathe. Loosen compacted soil so air can circulate to their roots, too.

Throw out wilted flowers.

Fresh flowers signify blossoming situations and, like live plants, they generate positive vibrations. But once they start to droop, throw them out—wilted blooms suggest decline and death.

> TIP: Flowers have long been associated with love—place a vase of fresh flowers in your Relationships Gua to brighten your love life.

Reduce the number of objects in a small room.

In a small room, quantity is even more important than size. Clutter really becomes apparent when space is limited. Rather than scaling down furnishings and accessories, dec-orate a small room with fewer pieces. This allows the eye to focus on what's really important instead of jumping around from item to item, which can be distracting and confusing.

Use larger pieces of furniture in a small room.
At first, this seems to go against logic. But if you place only a few small pieces of furniture in a small room (having already eliminated unnecessary furnishings and accessories), your room will either seem spartan or like a dollhouse. Larger objects give a small room a sense of drama, purpose, and stability.

Reposition furniture that obstructs access to a room.
A piece of furniture that blocks traffic into or through a room is an inconvenience to you and others—it also obstructs the smooth flow of ch'i. Move pieces that jut into pathways, interfere with opening doors, etc. If necessary, reduce the number of items in the room.

Hang artwork on a stairway wall.

Stairway walls tend to be underused as places to display artwork. Hanging pictures alongside stairs also attracts ch'i and encourages it to move up to the next story of your home, energizing your living environment on every level.

Use a consistent color scheme throughout your home.

Decorating each room with a different color scheme produces "color clutter" that can be psychologically jarring. If you use a consistent color scheme with only slight variations or accents of different hues, you'll create a sense of harmony throughout your home. This decorating trick also gives you greater versatility—you can move pieces from one room to another without the colors clashing.

Limit the number of colors in a room.

Although monochromatic decorating schemes can be boring, combining lots of different hues and patterns in a room may also produce color clutter. Limit your palette to three colors to create a sense of harmony. If you decide to include a variety of patterned objects in the same room, make sure they all contain the same colors so they seem related.

> TIP: Vary the size and type of the patterns you use together—small florals and broad stripes, for instance—so they don't compete with one another for your attention.

Organize hobby items neatly in the Creativity Gua.
Corral painting supplies, quilting materials, beer-making equipment, and so on in baskets, bins, or a trunk and store them in the Creativity Gua. This keeps hobby articles from spilling over into other parts of the home while simultaneously sparking your creativity.

Return borrowed items.
Is other people's stuff cluttering up your home? Return things you've borrowed from friends and neighbors promptly so they don't pile up in your living space. Because objects retain their owners' energies, other people's belongings may bring distracting vibes into your home.

Store sports equipment on racks.
Sporting goods can take up lots of space in your home. Use racks and hooks to hang up tennis rackets, golf clubs, bicycles, helmets, skates, etc., and keep them orderly. Each member of the family should assume responsibility for hanging up his or her own athletic equipment.

TIP: Get rid of tennis balls that have lost their bounce, golf balls with dings, and so on.

Mend holes in pockets.
Literally as well as symbolically, holes in the pockets of clothing allow money to slip away. Mend them!

Store suitcases inside one another.

Suitcases take up a lot of room. Store smaller suitcases inside larger ones when you pack them away—many luggage sets come sized this way intentionally.

> TIP: You can also store other items, such as off-season clothing, inside suitcases if your space is limited.

Share videos and DVDs with friends.

Although you may want to watch your favorite movies several times, you can reduce clutter in your entertainment area by sharing videos and DVDs with friends. Create a video library with close friends and family members rather than buying duplicate copies.

Buy underwear once a year.

Underwear tends to get bedraggled after a year or so. Replace it all in one shopping trip to save time, then throw out old undies or convert cotton ones to dust cloths. If you color-coordinate bras and panties, this practice allows you to match up items— colors may change from season to season. (A friend of mine throws out all her old underwear when a relationship ends and treats herself to new lingerie as a way of symbolically inviting new love into her life.)

Share rarely used items with friends.
How often do you use a punch bowl, picnic basket, or hedge trimmer? Consider sharing some of these rarely used items with friends or family members, rather than each of you purchasing your own. If it's convenient, you may wish to share the ownership and responsibility of larger items, too, such as vacuum cleaners or lawn mowers. This practice frees up storage space and saves everyone money.

Don't let clutter accumulate on your nightstand.
Clutter on your nightstand can produce confusion in your love life, because the bedroom is a private zone devoted to intimate activities. Bedroom clutter can also generate stress that may disturb your sleep—particularly when the clutter is near your head. You spend one-third of your life sleeping, so it's especially important to keep your bedroom clutter-free.

Vacuum under your bed.

Dirt and dust can aggravate allergies or other health problems and interfere with restful sleep. From the perspective of feng shui, dust acts as a magnet for stuck ch'i, which can lead to irritability, diminished vitality, and other complaints.

Don't store stuff under your bed.

Clutter under your bed blocks the smooth flow of ch'i and may disrupt sleep. Blocked ch'i can also produce confusion, obstacles, or stagnant conditions between you and a partner with whom you share the bed. If your living space is limited and you must utilize the area under your bed, be sure to neatly organize what you stash there. Pay attention to the symbolism attached to the items you place beneath your bed, too. Sharp objects, for instance, may produce subconscious feelings of discomfort that could disturb your sleep.

Dust bedroom furniture.
Has your love life lost its luster? Dust bedroom furniture and give it a fresh coat of oil or polish. This cure symbolically revitalizes your love life and helps to make it sparkle again.

> TIP: Think loving thoughts while you perform this cure.

Don't let your bedroom become a dumping ground.
If you allow all sorts of stuff to collect in your bedroom—ostensibly because you don't have anyplace else to put it—you create clutter that can cause distraction and confusion in a romantic relationship. Assess whether the articles you store in your bedroom are appropriate to the room's purpose. If not, find another location for them or consider getting rid of them.

Arrange your wardrobe to group similar items together.
Hang clothing so that similar items are grouped together and you won't have to search through your entire closet to locate a particular garment. Designate drawers for specific items—place garments you wear on the upper part of your body in the top drawers, and put jeans, shorts, etc., in the lower drawers.

Organize clothing according to frequency of use.
In your closet and dresser drawers, place items you wear frequently where you can access them conveniently. Hang or store "special occasion" garments in less accessible areas. If you always wear particular items together, hang them together.

Install clothing rods at various heights.
Garments hang at different lengths, so positioning clothing rods at varying heights increases the usable space in your closet. Instead of running a single rod the full length of a closet, install two rods, one above the other, to hold shorter items—shirts, jackets, vests, and skirts. Hang a full-height rod in only a portion of the closet for dresses, slacks, coats, and longer garments.

Group clothing by color.
This saves time by enabling you to see at a glance what goes with what. Odd items that don't match anything else will immediately stand out—get rid of these.

Place a small bell on your nightstand and ring it each time you enter your bedroom.
This simple ritual clears the air of unwanted vibrations that could interfere with your sleep. A bell can also act as a trigger and send a signal to your subconscious that it's time to relax. It can focus your attention on intimate matters, too, and may help you attract love into your life.

Smudge your home.
Smudging gets rid of bad vibes in your home that may be interfering with your health, wealth, or happiness. Clear the air by burning bundled sage or sage incense to purify the space and remove emotional clutter. This is especially important when you move into a new home or after an argument.

Smudge antiques and used objects to purify them.
Objects that have been owned by someone else can retain the vibrations of other people and places. Therefore, it's a good idea to cleanse antiques and other used items before letting them take up residence in your home. Use the smoke from burning incense or dried sage to smudge and purify preowned articles.

Open all the windows in your home periodically.
This clears the air and disperses stagnant energy along with atmospheric clutter that can build up in a closed space.

Evaluate bulk buying.
Buying in bulk may not be that good a deal if you have to find

room to store large quantities of items you won't use in a relatively short period of time. A better solution might be purchasing bulk products in common with family members or friends, so everyone saves money without incurring excess clutter.

~

Use old-fashioned coat trees.
Antique, standing coat trees can be a convenient and decorative way to keep hats and coats neat. If someone in the family suffers from closet phobia, put a coat tree in his or her bedroom. Use one in the bathroom to replace or augment towel bars.

~

Use comforters on beds.
Comforters facilitate bed making by reducing the number of sheets, blankets, etc., you need. You'll also cut down on the amount of dirty laundry you have to wash.

Wash sheets and put them back on the bed.

On laundry day, take the sheets off your bed and wash them. Instead of making the bed with a different set and folding and storing the freshly washed set, put the same sheets (now clean) back on your bed.

> TIP: On cold nights, make your bed with warm sheets fresh from the dryer.

Group objects in your Family Gua to encourage family unity.

Select an item to represent each member of the family and place these in a prominent spot in your Family Gua. Tie the objects together with a pretty red ribbon to symbolize togetherness (red is the color of good luck in China). Clear away from this area any items that suggest conflict, competition, unhappiness, or disruption.

~

Toss old love letters.
Holding on to letters from old flames can keep new love from entering your life. Discard reminders of past romances and you'll make room for new possibilities to come your way.

~

Throw out old postcards, invitations, date books, birthday cards, and other mementos.
Unless there's something truly precious about these markers from your past or you're planning to write your memoir, you probably don't need to hold on to them for the rest of your life. You'll still have your memories without the paper trail.

Organize photos in albums.

After weeding out the poor photographs, organize the keepers into albums, preferably in chronological order or by subject.

Remove photos of people other than you or your romantic partner from your bedroom.

Pictures of other people—friends, family members, etc.—draw your attention to them and distract your energy away from your romantic partner. Unclutter your bedroom of these photos and the emotional energy attached to them.

Save good photographs, dump bad ones.

Sort through old photographs and eliminate those that

aren't clear, flattering, informative, or special in some way. Dump pictures that don't favorably depict you and others, as well as any of people you don't remember or like.

~

Frame favorite photos.
Select your absolute favorite photographs and frame them. "Gallery" frames that group a number of photos within a single frame keep memories alive and can be great conversation starters. Or, use your imagination to create a photo collage.

~

Don't put a TV in your bedroom.
A TV brings influences from the outside world into your private space. This mental clutter can interfere with your love life or adversely affect your ability to sleep peacefully—especially if you watch the news or an upsetting or violent show before retiring. If you live in a studio apartment, cover the TV at night to minimize its influence.

~

Don't let dirty laundry collect in your bedroom.
Dirty laundry holds onto stale energy, which can have an adverse influence on your health and vitality. Don't let it mount up in your bedroom, where it can interfere with your well-being.

~

Groom pets regularly.
Especially in warm weather, pets can shed copious amounts of hair. To keep fur residue from collecting in your home, groom pets regularly—outside, if possible. This practice has side benefits, too. Studies have shown that petting an animal companion can reduce stress, and it also strengthens the bond between you and your pet.

Place four objects in your Wealth Gua.
Four is the number of permanence and security. If you have trouble holding on to money, choose four objects that symbolize wealth to you. Neatly arrange these in your Wealth Gua to help stabilize your financial situation.

Wash a window.
In feng shui, windows symbolize the eyes. Clean windows allow you to see a situation clearly. If you are experiencing confusion in a particular area of your life, wash the windows in the part of your home that corresponds to that area. (See Chapter Three for more information about the different gua and their associations.)

Clean screens.

Dirty screens cut down on the amount of light that comes through your windows. Ch'i enters your home via the windows, too, but dust-clogged screens prevent this life-giving force from reaching the interior. To maximize the light your home receives, it's important not only to wash the windows, but to keep screens clean as well.

Use salt to remove bad vibes.

Sprinkle a pinch of salt in the corners of your home to clear away disruptive or unwanted energies. Salt also protects your home from ambient bad vibes.

Divvy up cleaning chores with a partner or roommate.
One person may hate to vacuum, but not mind cleaning the bathroom. Another might enjoy cooking, but not like to wash dishes. Divide tasks with a partner or roommate according to individual preferences, so that each assumes a fair share of the housekeeping burden.

Sweep cobwebs from the corners of your home.
Cobwebs symbolize the past—sweep them away to remove stuck energy, attitudes, and emotions.

Collect loose change in a money jar.
Place a large, attractive jar in your Wealth Gua. Each time you drop a coin in the jar, concentrate on your intention to attract abundance. This practice lets you "prime the pump" and start prosperity flowing your way. When the jar is full, organize the coins, take them to the bank, and trade them in for paper money. Then start filling up your money jar again.

Organize receipts.
Use a box, expandable file, binder, or other convenient container for receipts. Organize receipts in clearly marked envelopes so you can find them easily. Arrange them by date, category, etc. Save receipts you'll need for tax purposes in one box, receipts for appliances or equipment with warranties in another, receipts for gifts or personal purchases you may have to return in another, and so on.

Corral cosmetics.
Keep cosmetics neat and orderly in trays, baskets, or containers with lots of small sections or dividers. Favorite items you use every day can stay in your medicine cabinet or in an attractive holder on your bathroom vanity. Move specialty products to another spot.

Discard old cosmetics.
Do you have a dozen lipsticks, but only use two or three favorite shades? Toss the rest to reduce clutter in your medicine cabinet. Old cosmetics can dry out or lose their effectiveness over time, too—if you haven't used it in six months, dump it.

Throw away old medications.
Outdated medications not only clutter your medicine cabinet, they may lose potency over time and become less effective. To reduce clutter and prevent potential health problems, throw away prescription and over-the-counter medications that have outlived their expiration dates.

Create "product consensus" among family members.
Although each member of your family may prefer—or need—certain specialized personal care products, you might be able to agree on some general-use items such as shampoo, soap, or toothpaste. Rather than cluttering up your bathroom with lots of different products, try to reach a consensus on as many items as possible.

Spark your creativity.

Neatly display three paintings, sculptures, or other works of art that you particularly like in your Creativity Gua, in order to spark your imagination. (*Three* is the number of creative activity and represents giving form to ideas.)

Make the most of vertical space.

Especially in small apartments where floor space and closets are at a premium, utilize the space at the top of a room. Expand your home's storage space with baskets, shelves, and racks hung above the fridge, chests of drawers, file cabinets, toilet, and so on.

Clean out your refrigerator.

Not only is spoiled food smelly and unhealthy, it clutters up your refrigerator. Cleaning out your refrigerator on a weekly basis makes it easier to find things, cuts down on waste, and prevents bacteria from building up. Rework leftovers into soups, stews, or casseroles.

> TIP: Place a paper towel under anything that might drip or spill, to minimize cleanup later.

Organize your refrigerator.

After you've disposed of old food, organize the contents of your refrigerator efficiently. Arrange similar products (such as lunch meats) or items you are likely to use together (like salad fixings) next to each other. Position perishable foods, such as fruits and vegetables, in the front of your refrigerator. Tall containers can be placed farther back, but keep small items where they are clearly visible so they don't get lost behind larger products.

Push chairs in after eating.
Get in the habit of pushing chairs back under the table after you leave it. They not only look neater that way, they also don't jut out into passageways, where they can cause stubbed toes and interfere with the smooth flow of ch'i through your home.

Buy lightbulbs in one or two wattages.
Rather than stocking up on an array of lightbulbs in every wattage, choose a couple of convenient options—maybe 60 and 100 watts—that will serve most of your lighting needs.

Wipe off containers.
Wipe off salad dressing bottles, condiments, juice containers, and other messy packages before you put them back in the refrigerator or cabinet.

Wipe up spills immediately.
Spills are inevitable in stoves and refrigerators. Wipe them up immediately, before they harden or burn into a formidable mess.

Clean your stove.
The Chinese believe that the stove generates wealth. Keep yours clean and in good working order to encourage prosperity.

Store large pans inside your stove.

If storage space is limited in your kitchen, store large iron skillets, cookie trays, etc., inside your stove.

> TIP: To keep the stream of prosperity flowing in your direction, turn on your stove's burners briefly each day, even if you don't actually cook anything.

Use gold coffee filters.

Gold coffee filters eliminate the need for paper ones. A single filter lasts a long time, and because gold doesn't interact with the coffee, your morning beverage actually tastes better.

Clean out under your kitchen sink.
Throw out old cleaning products that may have lost their effectiveness and move potentially harmful ones to a place where young children won't be able to reach them. To reduce clutter under your sink, buy cleaning products that have multiple uses.

Organize cleaning materials in a basket with a handle.
Organize assorted cleaning materials for floors, tile, windows, porcelain, and so on in a basket with a handle and store it under your kitchen sink. When you clean bathrooms, carry the basket with you—that way, you won't have to keep duplicate collections of cleaning products in different rooms.

Keep tools handy.
Collect basic, essential tools—a hammer and nails, screwdrivers, pliers, etc.—in a wire basket and keep it in a convenient place. If you don't have to search for the right tool, you're more likely to take care of minor repair jobs promptly.

Corral condiments.
Use a tray with handles to hold condiments you use regularly. This keeps them neat in your fridge or on a counter and makes it easy to carry all of them to the table together.

Give away books you've finished reading.
Although you might want to reread classics and a few favorite novels periodically, most books can be passed on to friends or donated to your local library after you've finished reading them. Reference texts you use frequently, autographed books, and those that have special significance can stay.

Organize books.
Whether you choose to group them by author, subject, or the Dewey decimal system, books should be organized on your shelves so they're easy to locate and look neat.

Organize magazines, journals, and newspapers.
Get rid of outdated periodicals so they don't continue to pile up. Holding on to "old news" can block new ideas from emerging. Recycle newspapers and take magazines to hospitals, nursing homes, or coin-operated laundries for others to read.

Utilize closet doors for storage.
Affix narrow shelves, racks, grids, hooks, or pegboards on the inside of closet doors to maximize storage space. (Remember to keep closet doors shut.)

Organize CDs, tapes, and records.
Categorize music by artist, genre, or another method to encourage easy access. Give away CDs, cassette tapes, and records you rarely listen to or trade them at a used music shop. Store the keepers in a convenient rack, drawer, or cabinet near your stereo system. Prune your music collection annually—if you haven't listened to it in a year, you probably don't need it.

Pay attention to objects that have special significance for you.
Enjoy your favorite objects—don't just let them sit there, collecting dust. When you use, admire, or otherwise appreciate your treasures, you invest them with positive energy and activate the intentions associated with them. Spotlight them in a place of honor in your home.

Use a laundry basket to hold stuff when traveling.
Toss odds and ends you want to take on a trip into a plastic laundry basket. You can carry the basket easily from room to room and from house to car. Last-minute items can be added without opening and repacking your suitcase.

Take a laundry basket to the pool or beach.
Lightweight and waterproof, plastic laundry baskets are great for holding beach or pool gear, too. Toys, towels, suntan lotion, sandals, snorkeling equipment, snacks, and so on stay neatly contained in the car en route and can be quickly packed up again when it's time to head home.

Provide a place for keys.
Instead of hunting for your keys, place hooks, a basket, or a bowl near your home's entrance to keep keys handy.

Discard old keys.
If you can't remember what a key fits and haven't used it in ages, get rid of it.

Clean out your attic.
The attic represents your mind and spiritual path. Cleaning up clutter in the attic makes room for new ideas and promotes mental clarity. This task, like cleaning your basement, can be broken down into small segments and accomplished over a period of time so it doesn't seem so intimidating.

Clean out your basement.
The basement symbolizes your subconscious. By cleaning out your basement, you address past conditions or repressed issues that may have been lingering in your subconscious. If this uncluttering task seems overwhelming, break it down into manageable components. For example, clean only a corner or section of your basement at a time.

Get rid of gifts you don't like or never use.
Just because you received something as a wedding present or housewarming gift doesn't mean you have to hold on to it forever. If you don't like it or never use it, pass it on to someone who will.

~

Discourage physical gifts from friends whose taste is different from yours.

Although friends and loved ones may mean well, sometimes their taste and yours just don't mesh. Instead of accepting gifts from them that you know you'll never use, ask them to donate money in your name to a favorite charity.

~

Give consumable gifts to friends.

Rather than buying friends and family members more stuff, give them consumable presents—concert or theater tickets, gift certificates to a favorite restaurant, gourmet foods, fancy soaps, etc. Treat them to something special they might not get to enjoy otherwise.

Furnish bedrooms with even-numbered items.
Odd numbers are associated with change, movement, and activity. If you place three or five pieces of furniture in a bedroom, you may generate restless energy that can disrupt sleep.

Empty ashtrays.
Ashtrays full of cigarette butts are not only unsightly, they also serve as magnets for stagnant ch'i. Empty them often. Stale, smoky air produces atmospheric clutter and stuck ch'i. Use an air filtration system or fans or open windows regularly to keep fresh air and healthy ch'i circulating through your home.

Empty wastebaskets.

Trash signifies old, cast-off stuff you no longer want or need. Pay attention to where you position wastebaskets by using the bagua, as discussed in Chapter Three. Empty them daily to prevent stuck ch'i from building up in your home.

Clear kitchen countertops of clutter.

According to feng shui, the kitchen is connected with prosperity. By keeping your countertops neat and orderly, you can reduce money-related stress and confusion. From a practical point of view, of course, uncluttered countertops allow you to work more efficiently. Place only the things you use every day on your kitchen countertops.

Hang cooking utensils above the stove.
Keep cooking utensils handy and neat by hanging them on hooks, a rack, or a magnetic strip above your stove or cooktop. If your stove is in an island, an overhead hanging rack provides a convenient place for storing cooking equipment.

Organize kitchen utensils and equipment according to their frequency of use.
View kitchen counters, drawers, and cabinets as high-priced real estate, and only store items there if you use them regularly. Place utensils and other equipment close to where they will be used—cooking items near the stove, cleaning products under the sink, preparation tools in cabinets and drawers at the prep counter, and so on.

Store dishes, accessories, gadgets, and appliances you rarely use away from your kitchen's primary work area.

Don't let highly specialized appliances and seasonal items you rarely use clutter up your kitchen. For example, rather than keeping pasta makers, fondue pots, and punch bowls in your kitchen cabinets, store them in a hall closet or other less accessible area.

Evaluate small appliances.

Small specialty appliances, such as bread makers, Crock Pots, and cappuccino makers, should be subjected to the same rigid standards as clothing—if you haven't used it in a year or more, ask yourself if you really need it. Many of these rarely used items take up more than their fair share of room in your kitchen. Consider passing them on to someone who'll use them more often.

Alphabetize spices.
Many spices come in nearly identical jars or tins. Alphabetical organization enables you to find what you need quickly and prevents you from grabbing the wrong one by mistake. Before you replace spices, assess your needs with a critical eye—it may not be space- or cost-effective to buy something you'll only use once a year.

Use hanging baskets for kitchen gadgets.
Especially handy in a small kitchen, hanging baskets offer a convenient and attractive way to corral gadgets such as corkscrews, bottle openers, potato peelers, wooden spoons, serving tools, etc.

Hang pots and pans.
Pots and pans are easily accessible when hung from an overhead rack, wall hooks, or a pegboard—especially in kitchens with limited cabinet space.

Store nonstick pans safely.
To keep nonstick (Teflon) surfaces from getting scratched, place a paper towel between pots and pans when you stack them in a cabinet, closet, or drawer.

Discard old spices.
Spices lose their potency over time. Throw out any that have been sitting around for too long.

Store recycling bins out of sight.

Like the contents of wastebaskets, recyclables symbolize things that have served their purpose and are now destined to leave your life. Put the bins in a spot where their clutter will not attract your attention and remind you of the past.

Remove odd socks from your dresser drawer.

Socks that have been separated from their mates for several weeks or more are probably destined to remain solo. Once a sock has lost its partner, remove it from your dresser drawer.

Turn single socks into dust cloths.
You don't have to toss odd socks—recycle them into dust cloths. Slip a soft cotton sock on your hand and use it to wipe down shelves, tabletops, and other furniture.

Use odd socks to clean mirrors and windows.
Odd cotton socks also make great cleaning cloths. Slip one on your hand and use it to wipe a mirror or window. As you clean, remember that windows and mirrors are symbolically linked with vision—washing them can help you to more clearly see a situation in your life.

Move sharp objects from your Relationships Gua.
Sharp or pointed objects can produce discomfort, cutting words, or harsh exchanges between you and a romantic partner. Don't place them in your Relationships Gua—move them to another spot to reduce arguments.

Change the decoration on your front door each season.
This gesture keeps your entryway looking pretty and up-to-date. It also acknowledges the changes in nature—and life—and helps you stay in step with the times.

Pare down Christmas tree ornaments.
Christmas tree ornaments and other holiday decorations are used only for a short period of time and can take up more than their fair share of space during the rest of the year. Sort through these seasonal items and weed out the ones that you don't really like or that don't have special meaning for you. Those you choose to keep will escalate in sentimental value.

Pack Christmas tree ornaments in coffee cans.
Protect fragile Christmas tree ornaments by wrapping them in tissue paper or bubble wrap and storing them in coffee cans. Label the cans so you know which ornaments are inside without having to unwrap them. Coffee cans are ideal for storing or shipping other breakables, too.

Divide work, living, and rest areas.

In small apartments, one room may serve multiple purposes. Separate your sleeping area from your living and work areas with a decorative screen, curtain, or other divider. It's hard to relax fully and put daytime tasks aside if a cluttered desk is nearby, reminding you of all the things you still have to do.

Update your address book.

This organizing cure works to improve your relationships with other people by causing you to focus on your connections with them and the roles they play in your life. Like all uncluttering cures, it also reduces confusion and saves time by making it easier for you to find addresses and phone numbers.

Have a yard sale.
Turn clutter into cash by holding a yard sale. This cure accomplishes two prosperity goals—making money and getting rid of clutter—simultaneously.

> TIP: To encourage family togetherness or neighborhood unity, hold a group sale—it's more fun, too.

Get rid of objects that have unpleasant associations for you.
Items that remind you of unpleasant experiences or people you don't like can be a subtle source of annoyance. Instead of letting them trigger negative thoughts and feelings, get rid of them.

Group pictures on walls.

Unclutter your walls by grouping paintings, photographs, etc., according to size, subject, style, or colors. Pictures in a variety of sizes and shapes can be hung in a pleasing arrangement that is itself a composition.

> TIP: Create a grid and sketch the configuration to scale on paper before you begin hammering nails into your walls.

Group decorative objects on a mantel, table, or shelf.
If you have many decorative objects you want to display, grouping them can prevent a cluttered appearance. Place similar items together. Because numbers have special meanings in feng shui, you may want to arrange objects in pairs to encourage cooperation, threes to stimulate action or change, or fours to promote stability. (See Chapter Three for more about number symbolism.)

Rotate artwork periodically.
If you have lots of artwork and can't display it all without creating a cluttered effect, rotate your art. Museums do this regularly to keep their collections fresh and exciting. Rotating artwork in your home prevents ch'i from getting stuck, too. Changing the pictures on your walls can also help you get a new perspective on a situation.

Rearrange furniture periodically.

To keep your life from becoming static, rearrange furnishings from time to time. One of the fundamental principles of feng shui is that when you make changes in your home, you spark changes in your life, too. Rearrange furniture in your bedroom to perk up your love life; move furniture in your living room to stimulate friendships.

> TIP: To keep changes manageable, move furniture around in one room or area at a time—too much change all at once can be unsettling.

Sketch a room to scale before buying furniture.

Measure your room and sketch it to scale before purchasing new furnishings. Note the locations of windows, doorways, stairs, heating and air-conditioning elements, and so on. You may think you know what will fit, but pieces don't look the same in a large showroom as they will in your home. Take the sketch with you when you go furniture shopping so you'll know if that terrific sofa or antique armoire will work in your space—you'll save time and money.

Keep your gua in mind when you buy new furnishings.

When you purchase new furniture, think about which gua it will occupy. Are the shape, color, function, and symbolism of the item compatible with the gua's meaning—and your intentions? For instance, if you are redecorating a room in the

Relationships Gua, you might want to include a pair of lamps, chairs, or nightstands instead of just one. Objects with curved lines encourage harmony when placed in the Family Gua, whereas sharp angles and straight lines tend to stimulate individual activity and tension.

Furnish your home with beds of the same size.
If possible, use the same size bed in each bedroom—all full or queen size, for instance. You won't have to purchase and store sheets in several different sizes, and you can easily interchange bedding as necessary. Buying linens in neutral colors or a single color palette will increase their versatility and allow you to reduce the number of sheets, blankets, etc., that you need.

Install a ceiling fan.
This cure stirs up sluggish ch'i while dispersing atmos-

pheric clutter, hot air, stuffiness, and unpleasant aromas in your home. Ceiling fans can also reduce heating and air-conditioning bills.

~

Turn clutter into art.
Scraps of old lace, antique buttons, foreign postage stamps, photos, odd earrings, seashells, and other bits and pieces can be combined into attractive collages. Use your creativity to transform miscellaneous clutter into works of art—then frame them in shadow boxes and hang them on your walls (preferably in your Creativity Gua).

~

Get rid of old paint cans.
After you paint a room or area of your home, it may be a good idea to keep a small amount of paint for touch-ups. Over time, however, your walls will change color slightly due to sun-

light, age, smoke, and other factors, so the paint in the can will no longer match. It also tends to dry up orseparate, rendering it unusable. Storing old paint might not be wise from a health perspective either, as some paints, varnishes, and finishes contain toxic substances. Cans of paint take up a lot of room, too—don't bother saving them for more than a year.

~

Place atlases and maps in your Travel Gua.
Atlases, books and magazines about foreign places, pictures of exotic locales, a globe, and other items that symbolize travel can open up opportunities for adventure if you organize them neatly in your Travel Gua.

~

Put things away as soon as you've finished using them.
Rather than letting stuff pile up, get in the habit of putting away clothes, books, CDs, games, etc., as soon as you've finished using them.

When you pick something up, do something with it.
Don't just relocate a magazine, your slippers, or a dish—put it where it belongs. Wash a dirty glass or file paperwork right away so you don't have to come back to it later on. Once you get in the habit of doing this, you'll find you don't waste as much time looking for things, either.

Fix something that has been annoying you.
From a practical perspective, this cure alleviates a condition that is a source of irritation to you—a clock that doesn't keep accurate time, a drawer that doesn't close properly, a cracked piece of tile. Symbolically, you are demonstrating your willingness to correct areas of your life that aren't as good as they could be.

Clean your fireplace or woodstove.

A dirty fireplace or woodstove is both inefficient and unsafe. In feng shui, the fire element is linked with growth, vigor, enterprise, and creativity. On a symbolic level, therefore, an ash-filled fireplace or stove can limit your vitality, enthusiasm, and good luck. Keep them clean and in good operation.

Vacuum heating ducts and elements.

Like fireplaces and woodstoves, heating systems are connected with vitality and growth. From the perspective of feng shui, vacuuming dust from heating ducts, vents, etc., allows more positive energy to circulate through your home. From a practical point of view, this cure will make your system function more efficiently and cut down on heating bills.

Establish a "temporary clutter" site.
Use a basket, plastic bin, box, or other container to temporarily hold clutter you can't deal with immediately. At least once a week, go through this container and organize or toss the contents to prevent a buildup of clutter.

Buy only what you need.
It can be tempting to buy something when it's on sale. But remember, a good deal is only a deal if you really need it and are going to use it soon.

Don't shop during the full moon.
During this lunar phase, we tend to behave impulsively and are more likely to buy things we don't really need. Unless you absolutely have to, don't go shopping around the time of the full moon—and make sure anything you buy on a whim can be returned.

CHAPTER FIVE

Control Clutter in Your Workplace

Make sure the entrance to your office or place of business is easily accessible and free of obstacles.
Your entrance gives visitors their first impression of you and your business—make it as neat and attractive as possible so it conveys a positive image. This is also where ch'i enters, bringing creative energy and prosperity with it. Clear any clutter, litter, or obstacles that could block the smooth flow of ch'i into your workplace. If your company is located in a building with

many other offices, do what you can to improve the main entrance to the building as well as the entrance to your own business.

~

Clean, polish, and repair the sign for your place of business. Like the entrance to your business, your sign conveys an image of your company to prospective clients. If it is dirty or in disrepair, people will get the impression that your business isn't sound or that you don't care about your work. Make sure your company's sign is attractive so clients—and helpful ch'i—will be drawn to you.

~

Clean up the sidewalk and street near your place of business. Litter and other clutter near your place of business creates an unsightly impression and can detract from your success. Don't just clean your entryway, take it a step further and tidy the surrounding areas, too.

~

Keep your waiting room clean and orderly.
The lobby or waiting room serves as a transition zone between the outside and inside of your workplace. Clients and customers develop their initial feelings about you and your business while sitting in your waiting room. Organize reading materials neatly, empty wastebaskets, dust tables, wash windows, and make sure furnishings are clean. (Clean restrooms are essential, too.)

~

Smudge your lobby, foyer, and waiting room.
Smudge public areas in your place of business each evening or first thing in the morning. This practice removes the vibrations

left by former clients and keeps them from influencing others. The preferred way to do this is by burning sage or incense, but you can also clear the air with aromatherapy light rings or diffusers that release cleansing scents (such as mint or citrus) into the area. It's a good idea to periodically smudge conference rooms and individual offices or cubicles, too.

~

Clear passageways through your work area.
When the paths through your work area are free of obstructions, you can move about easily in the space—and so can ch'i. An obstacle-free work space allows you to work more efficiently. Clear pathways also encourage prosperity because they allow ch'i to flow into all areas of the workplace, infusing them with life-giving energy.

Superimpose the bagua over your workplace.
Place the eight-sided bagua over a blueprint or floor plan of your workplace, just as you did with the floor plan of your home. Align the arrow at the center of the wall that holds the entrance to your place of business (or your own office entrance). Now you can see which areas of your workplace correspond to which parts of your professional life. (See Chapter Three for a diagram of the bagua.)

Answer e-mail promptly.
Keep e-mail from cluttering up your computer's memory. If you respond to e-mail as soon as you receive it, you'll clear your own memory, too.

Delete e-mail messages regularly, rather than storing them.
Cleaning out old e-mail is the electronic equivalent of eliminating old magazines, newspapers, and paper clutter. Delete messages as soon as you respond to them. If you want to save messages, create a special file for old e-mail, and prune it regularly.

Answer snail mail promptly.
Don't allow correspondence to pile up—it not only clutters your desk, it also serves as a nagging reminder of unfinished business. Rather than wasting time rereading mail and memos several times, deal with them promptly. When you open a letter, reply to it and then file it or throw it away.

Replace burned-out lightbulbs in your office or work area.
In feng shui, light symbolizes the sun and helps to stimulate
positive energy and growth. Burned-out light bulbs diminish
vitality and can cause finances and/or business opportunities to
languish. Kee p your financial picture bright by replacing lightbulbs as soon as they burn out. In some cases, you may wish to
replace a bulb with one of a higher wattage to increase the
amount of energy being generated in a particular area.

Dust, clean, and polish your cash register.
If your place of business has a cash register, make sure it's clean and sparkling. Dust, grime, chipped paint, and corrosion discourage positive ch'i and can hamper your cash flow.

TIP: Put your cash register in the Wealth Gua of your business to stimulate prosperity. Tie a red ribbon on it and put three *I Ching* coins in your cash drawer for good luck.

Return phone calls.
Like the previous cures, this one clears up lingering obligations and gets them out of your way so you can stop thinking about them and move ahead. Returning phone calls promptly also demonstrates good manners and respect for callers.

Take care of notes on self-stick paper.
These constant reminders of things you haven't taken care of yet can distract you from the task at hand. Lots of little notes stuck all over your office can also make you feel inefficient or overwhelmed by unfinished business. Tend to them quickly, rather than letting them clutter up your office—you'll improve your productivity and your sense of accomplishment as a result.

Utilize money and resources wisely.
Eight is the number of pragmatism, business, and finance. Place eight objects in the Wealth Gua of your workplace to encourage the practical utilization of money and other resources. Make sure the items you choose signify your intentions.

Clear your in-box.

Like the previous cure, this one reduces paper clutter that can distract you and diminish your productivity. Get in the habit of clearing your in-box by the end of each day. Completing this task enables you to be more efficient and stay on top of work-related issues.

> TIP: If you can't handle everything in your in-box right away, consider using two in-boxes, one for stuff that needs to be addressed ASAP and one for less-pressing paperwork. But don't let things pile up in the second box!

Remedy a missing gua in your office.

If your office or work space is irregularly shaped and has a notched-out section or a missing gua, you may be missing out on moneymaking opportunities. Hang mirrors on the walls of the missing corner to cut symbolic windows in these walls (see Chapter Three for more information). This cure opens up your space so your prosperity isn't limited.

Remove old files and documents from your computer.

Pruning your computer of files and documents you no longer need makes it easier to find what you want. It also frees up space on your hard drive and speeds your computer's operation.

Group computer documents into as few folders as possible.
Set up a few subject categories and organize documents into subcategories within the main subject groups. This makes it easier to find documents and keeps your computer desktop neat.

Back up your computer work regularly.
It's amazing how many people overlook this simple task. If your computer fails (or is stolen), you won't have to waste valuable time redoing lost work. At the end of each day, or when you finish working on a particular project or document, back it up on a zip disk, compact disc, or floppy. Keep a backup disk of important work in a place outside your office—at home, in a safe-deposit box, or in another location.

Use plants to absorb emotional and mental clutter.
When many people must work together in tight quarters, place plants between desks to provide a sense of privacy. Plants also absorb the energies emitted by many workers, reducing stress. In feng shui, plants are a favorite cure because they symbolize growth—encourage growth in your business by including a number of live plants in your office decor.

TIP: Remember to keep plants neatly trimmed and healthy—dead leaves signal decay and decline.

In an open office plan, group desks so everyone is comfortable.

Ideally, everyone should be seated so that he or she can clearly see the entrance to the room. This prevents workers from being startled or distracted by someone walking up behind them. In an open office situation that includes many desks, the ideal arrangement may not be possible. If some individuals must be seated with their backs to the door, position mirrors so they can see the reflection of the entrance without having to turn around.

Update your contact list.

Do you have piles of business cards stuffed in your address book or wallet? Are names and phone numbers scrawled on slips of paper? Update your contact list regularly so you can find names, addresses, and phone numbers easily and do away with paper clutter. You'll also reduce the risk of losing someone's address or number.

~

Limit wooden objects to control growth.

Usually growth in a business is desirable, but growth that occurs too rapidly may be stressful or problematic. To control the rate of growth and create stability, move some wooden items out of the Self and Future Guas of your workplace. Replace them with metal ones, which symbolize structure. If, at a later date, you want to spark growth again, you can put the wooden pieces back. Experiment until you get the right mix to produce balance.

~

Get rid of metal objects to encourage flexibility.

The element of metal is associated with structure and rigidity.

If you want to encourage spontaneity, change, and flexibility in your business—or the people who work there—reduce the number of metal items in the work area. Replace metal desks with wooden ones, for instance, to stimulate growth and new opportunities.

Adjust doors in your work area so they open and close easily.

Doors that don't work properly impede the flow of ch'i through your workplace and can limit your prosperity. The door of your main entrance and doors in your Wealth Gua are the most crucial, but ill-fitting doors in any area can cause obstacles. Plane the edges of doors that stick, oil hinges, fix wobbly knobs, and so on so that everything operates easily.

Organize your supply closet.

Organize office supplies and arrange them according to use—group computer supplies together, mailing materials together, etc. Get rid of supplies you won't be using anymore when you update your office equipment or switch to other products. Place items you use often in easily accessible spots.

Clear your Future Gua to encourage new business.

The number *one* represents new beginnings. To stimulate new opportunities, remove all but one significant item from the Future Gua of your work space. Make sure the object you choose to leave there has positive associations and is compatible, from a symbolic standpoint, with your goals, business, or future plans.

Don't store old stuff in your Future Gua.

A storage closet or file cabinet full of old business can stifle growth and block new opportunities if it's in the Fame/Future Gua of your workplace. Clutter in this area can also cause other people to have a distorted or confused image of your business. Clear away anything that doesn't point to the future and encourage positive associations.

~

Block out time segments on your calendar.

It may not be enough to just write down an appointment on your calendar or in your date book. To see at a glance how much time you really have available in a day, block out segments with different colored high-lighter pens to clearly show what portion of your day each commitment actually takes up. If a meeting (including the time spent commuting) will occupy two hours, color in a quarter of the calendar's square for that day. This practice helps you keep from over-booking yourself.

~

Color-code appointments on your calendar.

Design a system of colors to prioritize your appointments, such as red for essential or ASAP, blue for less important or ongoing projects. This method lets you see at a glance what you need to take care of first and helps you to organize your time more effectively.

~

Clean off your desk at the end of each day.

This practice lets you put your tasks "to bed" at the end of the workday. It also gives you a chance to catch anything that might have been misplaced or accidentally shoved under a pile of paperwork. In the morning, a clean desk invites you to start fresh, without feeling overwhelmed by tasks left over from yesterday.

~

Place only items you use regularly on your desktop.
Think of the top of your desk as the most valuable piece of real estate in your office. Only those things that you use in your daily routine, such as your computer, telephone, contact list, and message pad, should be allotted this precious desktop space.

~

Superimpose the bagua on your desktop.
You can superimpose the octagon-shaped bagua over your desktop, just as you did with a floor plan of your workplace. This enables you to see which portion of your desk relates to which sector of the bagua. When you are seated at your desk,

the far right-hand section describes your business relationships. The far left-hand part corresponds to money, the area to your near right signifies travel as well as people who can help you, and so on. Use this method to organize your desk and your work life. (Refer to the diagram of the bagua in Chapter Three.)

~

Use the eastern section of your desk for new business.
The east, where the sun rises, is considered the point of new beginnings, so this can be a good spot to keep file folders, correspondence, and other materials that relate to new projects. Go through this paperwork daily to stay current. Move "in progress" materials to a different area. This keeps clutter from accumulating and makes room for new opportunities to continue flowing into your life.

Hang bins or baskets in your office.
Hang baskets or wood, metal, or plastic bins on the walls in your office to reduce desktop clutter and keep paperwork handy.

Rearrange objects on your desk periodically.
This cure stirs up new possibilities and prevents your work situation and finances from growing stagnant. It also gives you a chance to reevaluate items—which ones do you really need and which are less important and can be moved off your desktop? In the process, you might even find something you thought was lost forever!

Organize cosmetics in a pencil holder.
Small cosmetics, such as lipstick, eyebrow pencil, and mascara, stay neatly organized in the compartments of a pencil tray. Choose one that's designed to attach inside a desk drawer or a portable pencil holder like the ones kids use for school.

Organize small office supplies in a convenient desk drawer.
Rather than letting tape, self-stick notes, a stapler, paper clips, etc., clutter your desktop, move them to an easily accessible desk drawer. Corral loose items in an organizing tray, basket, or other sectioned holder to keep them from shifting around in the drawer.

Use an area rug to unite furniture.

To reduce the cluttered appearance of many pieces of furniture—especially in a small office or waiting room—place an area rug so that each piece of furniture rests partly on the rug. This decorating cure has an added advantage, too. By establishing visual unity, it symbolically brings together the different elements in the room and promotes workplace harmony.

TIP: A round or oval rug encourages cooperation, a rectangular one promotes growth, a square one increases stability.

Organize books, magazines, and reading materials.
Arrange books, trade magazines, and other reading or reference materials in a logical, convenient manner—by subject, title, date, author, or whatever method works best for you.

Discard outdated reference materials.
Recycle or discard old trade magazines and reference materials that you no longer use. Old literature not only creates clutter, it also can keep you stuck in the past and interfere with the flow of new ideas and information.

Rearrange items on a table or shelf in your Wealth Gua.
If your company's finances are sluggish, rearrange the objects on a shelf, table, or other piece of furniture in the Wealth Gua of the president or CEO's office (or the office of another principal). Whenever you make a change like this in a section of your workplace, you spark change in the corresponding area of your business. This cure helps get your cash flow moving again.

Place reading materials in the Wisdom/Knowledge Gua.
Organize books, magazines, trade journals, reference texts, and other reading materials in the Knowledge Gua of your office to stimulate the flow of information and ideas.

Keep a notepad handy to record ideas.

Many people get bright ideas when they're walking, driving, waiting in line, or performing mindless, routine tasks. Carry a notepad with you to jot down brainstorms and inspirations, so they don't get lost in the clutter of your daily work demands.

Put away file folders promptly.

How much time do you waste searching for files that weren't put away promptly or properly? As soon as you finish with a file, put it back so you and others can find it easily. In an office where many people share common file cabinets or materials, this organizing task becomes even more imperative.

Clean off a shelf in the top of a closet.
A cluttered overhead shelf in a closet suggests that you have problems hanging over your head. This condition can lead to stress or headaches—something might even fall from the shelf and hit you on the head! Get rid of things you aren't using and neatly organize the rest.

Work on one project at a time.
Don't try to juggle several projects simultaneously—it's inefficient, confusing, and stressful. Focus on one thing at a time—keep files and materials related to other tasks storedaway until you're ready to devote your attention to them. This also prevents paperwork from getting misfiled.

Follow through.
Allow enough time to finish a project once you start it. Follow through until you complete a task, or a designated portion of it. Each time you have to set work aside and come back to it, you clutter your mind with other thoughts and waste time refocusing your attention.

Place pairs of objects in the Relationships Gua.
This cure is especially valuable if you work in partnership with someone, but it can also improve interactions among coworkers. In the Relationships Gua of your workplace, arrange objects in pairs. Two is the number of cooperation, congeniality, and teamwork, so placing two chairs, two lamps, two pictures, etc., in this gua can have a positive effect on all business relationships.

Rein in electrical cords.

Some office systems are designed with channels to keep electrical cords hidden. In other cases, you can rein in cord clutter by tying them together neatly with rubber bands or twist ties.

Attract financial help from someone else.

Six is the number of shared resources. To attract financial help from a partner, investor, bank, or other source, clear away all but six items from the Wealth Gua of your work space. The symbolic quality of these objects is important, too, so pay attention to the meanings attached to those that remain—they should have positive, prosperous associations for you.

> TIP: One of the six items could be a light or a live plant, as both cures encourage growth.

Keep business meetings on track.
Create an agenda for meetings and stick to it. Don't allow dis-
cussions to wander off track. Rather than bringing in side issues
that can clutter your focus and detract from the main points
under consideration, schedule another meeting to deal with
those concernslater.

Clean light fixture covers.
Dusty lampshades and light fixture covers cut down on the
amount of light—and ch'i—flowing into your work space.
Electric lights symbolize the sun, growth, clarity, and vitality.
Increased light equates with a brighter financial picture and
better overall well-being for your business.

Wash the phone in your office.
From a practical standpoint, this helps to keep germs from spreading—especially if more than one person uses your office phone. Symbolically, washing your phone suggests that you are striving for clear communication with business associates and clients.

Wash the windows in your office.
Ch'i enters a building through its windows. Clean windows let more light and positive energy into your work area, thereby improving your financial prospects and your firm's general well-being. Because windows represent a building's eyes in feng shui, clean windows allow you to see situations more clearly—symbolically as well as physically.

Arrange ceramic items in your Wealth Gua to stabilize finances.
If money seems to go out as fast as it comes in, neatly arrange objects made of a ceramic material—tile, pottery, brick, stone—in the Wealth Gua of your workplace.

> TIP: To make this cure even more effective and improve money management at the same time, place four ceramic objects in your Wealth Gua and hang a mirror behind them.

Clean your computer screen.
This practical maintenance cure not only enables you to see your work more easily, it reinforces your intention to make the most of your income-producing capability. Dust on your computer screen can physically and symbolically interfere with your

ability to clearly see the task before you. The more you use your computer, the more important this becomes—dust its screen daily.

~

Remove old files and paperwork from your desk and file cabinet.
Cluttering up drawers with old files can block moneymaking opportunities. Remove old materials that may be keeping you stuck in the past to make room for new business to come your way.

~

Remove sharp objects from the Relationships and Helpful People Guas of your office.
Scissors, letter openers, and other sharp objects placed in the Relationships Gua or the Helpful People Gua of your office can have a detrimental effect on your relationships with coworkers, colleagues, and clients. Sharp or pointed items symbolize

cutting words, backstabbing, severed ties, and other hurtful conditions. Move these tools to another spot.

~

Clean out your briefcase.

This cure is similar to cleaning out your desk or file cabinet, but it can be even more important for people whose work requires them to travel or conduct business outside of the office. Remove clutter from your briefcase to make room for new business and moneymaking opportunities. Get rid of old paperwork, names and addresses of people you no longer contact—anything you don't use or need.

~

Color-code computer floppy disks, CDs, and zip disks.

Organizing diskettes and CDs into subject categories by color enables you to quickly find the one you want.

Color-code file folders.

File folders can be organized according to subject or category, too. Using a color-coding system makes it easy to see at a glance what's in a crowded file drawer—it can also help you to spot outdated or misplaced files. Color-coding can be used in conjunction with other filing systems—alphabetical, chronological, etc.

Throw away pens that don't write.

How many times have you grabbed a pen to jot down a message only to discover that it's out of ink or clogged? Instead of putting it back where it will annoy you again, throw it away.

Use pencils with retractable lead.
Pencils with retractable lead never need to be sharpened, so they don't produce messy shavings. Whether you prefer disposable ones or distinctive refillable mechanical pencils, they are cleaner and more convenient than ordinary wooden pencils.

Organize "bright ideas" in index-card file boxes.
Store ideas for future projects in index-card boxes. Use a different box for each project and label or color-code them. Write only one thought on a card. File cards according to categories, such as financial info, marketing tips, etc. You can easily rearrange, add, and remove cards as your project develops. But don't just stick your brainstorms in a box and forget about them—go through the boxes at least once a week. Weed out ideas after implementing them. Toss those that you've decided not to use and act on those that still seem promising.

Use a blackboard for daily reminders.

Rather than posting lots of little notes around your office, use a blackboard instead. This keeps paper clutter to a minimum and encourages you to respond to messages promptly. A blackboard also cuts down on waste and saves trees.

> TIP: Use different-colored chalks to prioritize messages.

Complete a task on your to-do list.

Unfinished tasks produce mental clutter and nag at you, making you feel ineffectual. Each time you complete a task, you experience a sense of satisfaction at having taken charge of your life and alleviated one more obstacle to your happiness. Make a to-do list at the start of each day and strive to eliminate as many items as possible—at least three, preferably ten or more.

Hang a wind chime between your workplace and an obtrusive building.

If you feel pressured by a neighboring building that's too close or much larger than yours, hang a wind chime in the window between your office and the other building. The movement and pleasing sounds of the chimes disperse the disruptive atmospheric clutter and tension produced by the obtrusive structure and its occupants.

Don't place a wastebasket in your Wealth Gua.

You may end up "throwing away" your money on things you don't need or unprofitable ventures if you put a wastebasket in the Wealth Gua of your office. Move it!

Keep wastebaskets hidden or in unobtrusive spots.
Trash represents things you don't want or need. To prevent workers from paying too much attention to things that are no longer useful, place wastebaskets where they aren't obtrusive.

Install fans to circulate positive ch'i.
The windows of many large office buildings, warehouses, and other structures don't open to let fresh air circulate. As a result, ch'i can stagnate. Ceiling fans stir up stuck ch'i and disperse atmospheric clutter to reduce stress, stimulate new ideas, and promote healthy interaction between workers.

Eliminate sharp angles to improve communication.

Lots of straight lines and sharp angles in your workplace tend to increase single-mindedness and can interfere with give-and-take between coworkers. To improve communication and cooperation, remove objects with sharp corners or many angles, especially in the Relationships and Helpful People Guas.

> TIP: Place a few glass objects here to facilitate communication between coworkers, clients, and colleagues.

Keep lunchrooms and break areas neat.

These areas are intended as oases from the stress of the workplace, but if they are cluttered or dirty, they may have the opposite effect. Workers who can clear their minds periodically throughout the day tend to be more productive at their jobs. Messy break areas can also contribute to low morale, arguments, and general confusion, so keep these rooms neat, clean, and attractive.

~

Ring a bell upon entering your office.
The sound of the bell summons positive ch'i into your office and clears the air of unwanted vibes that can produce atmospheric clutter. This simple ritual can also serve as a trigger to stimulate your intention to get down to work and generate income.

~

Vacuum your office.
Vacuum or sweep your office floor at the end of each day. Then, when you enter your office in the morning, you'll symbolically step into a fresh environment full of opportunity. Because rugs and floors represent foundations, a floor that's free of dirt and clutter suggests an orderly, stable base under your feet.

Create a focal point in your office or work space.
When your mind starts to wander, use a focal point to bring your attention back to your objective. Clutter distracts and scatters your attention; a focal point hones and directs it. Choose something attractive—a picture, a vase of flowers, a meaningful item—as your focal point. If your objective is to earn more money, place the focal point in the Wealth Gua of your workplace. If your reputation and public image are of primary importance, create a focal point in your Fame/Future Gua.

Create a focal point in a waiting room.
Give clients and visitors something to focus on while they wait, to help keep their minds from wandering to other things. This focal point should be something that encourages positive feelings about your company and conveys beneficial energy. A large, healthy plant or floral arrangement, a tank full of

colorful fish, attractive artwork, and handsomely framed inspirational sayings are a few possibilities.

~

Clear clutter from your Travel Gua.
Clutter in your Travel Gua can cause confusion, delays, and mix-ups when traveling. To facilitate smooth and profitable business trips, make sure this sector in your workplace is neat and orderly.

> TIP: Organize materials related to travel—as well as those that your company uses in connection with shipping and receiving—in this gua.

~

Use calming scents in your office or work area.
Soothing aromas, such as vanilla and lavender, can cut through mental clutter and help you stay calm under pressure.

Depending on your office environment, you can burn incense, stash fragrant potpourri or a sachet in a drawer, or dab your wrists with essential oil to reduce stress and mental clutter.

~

Use stimulating scents to improve mental clarity.
The refreshing scents of citrus and mint can help to keep you alert and increase mental clarity. Use these aromas in your personal space or diffuse them throughout your office environment to chase away sluggishness, stimulate the flow of new ideas, and improve communication between workers.

~

Hire help when you need it.
Although you may prefer to do everything yourself—or feel that you should—sometimes it pays to hire other people to help out. Overloading yourself with tasks can cause stress and

burnout. It may not even be cost-effective if low-level functions are taking up time and energy you could be devoting to more important ones.

CHAPTER SIX

Control Clutter Outside Your Home

Superimpose the bagua over your yard.
Place the eight-sided bagua over a plot plan or sketch of your property, just as you did with the floor plan of your home's interior. Align the arrow at the center of the yard's border that bears the driveway, sidewalk, or entrance to your property. Now you can see which areas of your yard correspond to which parts of your life. (See Chapter Three for a diagram of the bagua.)

Trim shrubs and trees near your home's entrance.

Plants give off positive vibrations and are usually considered assets. But if they are overgrown, they can obstruct the flow of ch'i to your home and limit its beneficial energy. Remove dead leaves and branches from trees and shrubs near your home to prevent an image of death and decay. From a practical perspective, keeping dead limbs neatly trimmed will prevent them from falling on power lines, damaging your property, or perhaps causing an injury.

Recycle.

Recycle everything you can. This eco-friendly practice reduces clutter in our world, to everyone's advantage.

Buy recycled products.
Recycling waste is only half the solution to the ever-expanding buildup of garbage in our world. When you buy products made from recycled materials, you support efforts to decrease waste and encourage companies to seek environmentally friendly solutions.

Clean up the sidewalk and street near your home.
Accumulated trash, dead leaves, and other debris make the area around your home unsightly and can interfere with the smooth flow of ch'i. Clear away this clutter to create a positive first impression of your home and community, and to improve relationships with neighbors.

Fix cracked or broken pavement in a driveway or sidewalk.
Like many feng shui cures, this one has both a practical and a symbolic side. Repair a damaged sidewalk or driveway to encourage the smooth flow of ch'i to your home and to prevent accidents.

Use the bagua to analyze an apartment building.
If you live in an apartment building, position the bagua over a plan of the entire building by aligning the arrow with the main entrance. Although your own apartment has a more direct influence on your life than the common areas, the building in which you live will also affect you. For instance, cleaning up the entrance to your apartment building can help prevent problems with neighbors and present a positive image to passersby.

Corral garden tools.
Store small tools in a bucket or basket with a handle. This keeps them together and makes them easy to transport.

Weed your garden.
Weeds suggest that problems are choking your personal growth and limiting your good fortune. Pull them out to remove impediments to your happiness. Weeds also obscure flowers and deprive them of nutrients—get rid of them so you can showcase your favorite plants.

Make a statement in your Self/Identity Gua.
Clear away anything in your Self/Identity Gua that doesn't represent you. Then make this area as distinctive and beautiful as possible—plant flowers, install attractive lighting, etc. If your mailbox is in this gua, decorate it with positive images from your life (for example, if you enjoy sailing, paint boats on it). If your front door falls in your Self Gua, paint it a bright, cheerful color (red is considered lucky in feng shui) and affix handsome brass numerals to the door.

Rake your yard.
This uncluttering cure improves the outer appearance of your home and makes it more attractive to visitors and ch'i. Because fallen leaves symbolize death and decay, it's a good idea to promptly remove them from your yard.

Cut the grass.
Neatly trimmed grass adds to your home's visual appeal and attracts positive ch'i. An overgrown yard symbolizes tasks or problems that are growing out of control. Keep grass neatly trimmed to get a handle on challenges in your life and to present a positive image to passersby.

Fill in a missing gua with symbolic corners.
If your home is missing a gua, fill in the gap with a symbolic corner outside (see Chapter Three for more information). Place an object—a plant, flagpole, light, birdbath, or wind chime, for instance—where the missing corner *would* be positioned if you visually extended the walls of your house.

Encourage kids to pick up toys.
Toys strewn about the yard, porch, or driveway create an unsightly appearance that symbolizes confusion and carelessness. In some cases, scattered toys may even cause accidents. Encourage children to pick up their toys after they've finished using them.

~

Clean gutters.
Clogged gutters symbolize stagnant conditions and obstructions in your life. Unblock gutters so water—and ch'i—can flow freely.

Replace burned-out lights.
From a practical perspective, good lighting outside your home allows you and your visitors to see clearly and prevents accidents. In feng shui, light symbolizes the sun's life-giving energy. Replace burned-out lights, especially at the entrance to your home, to attract ch'i and its benefits.

Clean out your garage.
Like other uncluttering cures, this one helps you to eliminate confusion, obstacles, and old behavior patterns and habits. It also clears the way for new opportunities and good luck to enter your life. Break this task down into manageable components so you don't become overwhelmed—or get the whole family involved.

Organize a neighborhood cleanup project.

Get neighbors together to clean up litter and natural debris in your area. A group endeavor not only makes the work go quicker, it gives you an opportunity to strengthen relationships with neighbors and demonstrate pride in your community.

Clean out your car, including the trunk.

Clutter in your car can cause confusion, delays, obstacles, and other problems when you travel. Clean your car, inside and out, to facilitate both local and long-distance trips. The more time you spend in your car, the more important this cure is.

Organize your glove compartment.
Like the previous cure, this one encourages safe, smooth travel. It also helps you to find important materials (such as your registration) and safety equipment (flashlight, tire gauge, ice scraper, etc.) when you need them.

Smudge your car's interior.
Perform this cure any time you feel a need to disperse disruptive energies from your car, such as after a particularly stressful trip or an accident. It's a good idea to smudge a car when you buy it, too, especially if someone else owned it previously, to remove other people's vibes. Burn sage or pine incense in the ashtray to clear away unwanted energies and purify the interior of your vehicle.

Use a net or screen to organize your trunk.
Nets or screens designed to fasten in your trunk keep stuff from sliding around when you drive. They also compartmentalize handy tools, supplies, and other gear that permanently reside in your trunk.

Put a litter basket in your car.
Keep a litter basket or trash bag handy in your car—and use it. Empty it daily to keep clutter from accumulating in your car.

Organize maps.
Neatly fold and organize road maps according to region, so you can quickly find the one you need when traveling. Throw out outdated maps and replace them with current ones to avoid confusion.

Keep tapes and CDs neat in your car.
Organize cassette tapes and CDs in a carrying case or other compartmentalized container so you can find the one you want to listen to quickly and easily. Searching for a particular tape or CD while driving can distract you and could be dangerous. Keeping your music in a special carrying case also lets you conveniently transport your favorite tapes and CDs between your car and home.

Organize loose change.
Use a coin holder in your car to organize loose change and keep it handy for tolls, parking meters, etc.

Use pet guards in your car.
Allowing pets to jump around in the car while you drive is dangerous—for them and for you. If you regularly travel with pets, keep them safely restrained and away from the driver by installing pet guards. Use carrying cages with attached food and water dishes for short or occasional trips.

Eliminate straight lines and sharp angles in a garden.
Gardens are oases where we go to find peace and relaxation. Straight lines and sharp angles, however, symbolize rapid movement and activity and can produce stress instead of tranquility. Nature doesn't form straight lines or right angles—follow her lead and design your garden with graceful curves.

Hang a wind chime between your home and electrical power lines.

To counteract the unwanted effects of electromagnetic frequencies (EMFs) from power lines, hang a wind chime between your home and the electrical lines. This cure disperses stress-producing EMFs that can clutter your environment and circulates them away from your home.

Hang a wind chime between your home and a noisy neighbor.

A wind chime can also disperse the disruptive influence of a noisy neighbor. Hang one between your home and theirs to chase away atmospheric clutter and its disturbing effects.

Move noisy objects out of the Relationships Gua of your property.
Noisy objects and equipment, such as lawnmowers and power saws, can cause friction between you and a partner if you store them in the Relationships Gua of your property. Move them to another location.

Hang a bagua on a door that faces a busy street.
If you live on a busy or noisy street, hang a bagua on the door facing the street to reflect noise and disruptive energy away from your home. This cure helps prevent atmospheric clutter and the resulting stress from adversely impacting the inhabitants of your home.

Put a recycling bin near mailboxes in an apartment building.
If you live in an apartment building, you can keep fliers and junk mail from accumulating and cluttering the entryway to your building by setting a recycling bin near the mailboxes. This cure makes it easy for residents to discard junk mail and other unwanted paper.

Bury money to attract prosperity.
Fill a small, rectangular cardboard box with coins and tie a red ribbon around it, rectangles symbolize growth; red is a lucky color in feng shui. Then "plant" the box by burying it in the Wealth Gua of your property to attract prosperity.

Pay attention to the location of garbage cans.
Trash represents things in your life that you are ready to release. Notice which gua your garbage can occupies. If it is located in your Wealth Gua, you may be throwing away your money. If you put it in your Relationships Gua, you could be dumping garbage into your love life.

Arrange patio furniture outside to fill in a missing gua in your home.
You can compensate for a missing gua in your home's floor plan by arranging patio furniture outside the house, in the space where the missing sector should be. This cure visually extends the footprint of your home and invites activity into the part of your life represented by that gua.

Stack wood to encourage growth.
In feng shui, wood symbolizes growth and expansion. If you use wood in a fireplace or woodstove, stack it neatly in the gua that represents an area of your life in which you want growth to occur.

Hang prayer flags to promote peace.
Buddhists traditionally hang colorful flags printed with prayers and blessings outside their homes and temples. When the wind blows, it carries the blessings to other beings around the world. You can write your own good wishes on colorful pieces of cloth and tie them to a pole, tree, clothesline, etc., to promote peaceful, positive conditions in your environment.

CHAPTER SEVEN

Clutter Control for Kids

Get kids involved in clutter control.

Encourage children to unclutter their rooms. Clutter in children's bedrooms can increase hyperactivity, distraction, frustration, and confusion. It also puts obstacles in their way. "A chaotic sea of stuff and inappropriate storage options can disrupt children's lives at every stage of development," explains Lisa Skolnik in her book *The Right Storage*. Toy chests, shelves, baskets, colorful plastic tubs, etc., make it easy for them to put away games and toys after playing with them. Help kids appreciate the value of putting their stuff away so they can find it the next time they want it.

Don't let kids think you're their personal maid.
Get kids in the habit of picking up after themselves from an early age, so they don't expect maid service from you or others later on in life. Organizing personal belongings has a direct relationship to organizing thoughts, and tidying up improves a child's ability to think clearly and logically. Studies suggest that children who grow up in neat, orderly environments tend to do better in school and be more successful as adults.

Place books in the Knowledge Gua of a child's room.
Neatly organizing books in this sector of a child's bedroom encourages learning and can improve his or her schoolwork.

Give kids their own bulletin boards.

Clean clutter off your refrigerator door by giving kids personal bulletin boards for displaying their artwork, class schedules, reading lists, souvenir photos, after-school activities info, and so on. Hang the bulletin boards in their bedrooms to help them organize their lives and celebrate themselves at the same time.

Recycle kids' toys.

When children outgrow their toys, pass them on to friends' younger children or donate them to charity. Holding on to outdated objects shows a reluctance to release the past and embrace the future.

Don't put a TV in the Knowledge Gua of a child's room.
If you place a television set in the Wisdom/Knowledge Gua of a child's room, you encourage him or her to glean too much information from this single source. Instead, organize books, encyclopedias, atlases, and a variety of other learning tools in this sector to stimulate intellectual growth.

Keep toy collections from growing out of control.
Each time a child receives a new toy, instruct him or her to give away an old one. Let the child decide whether to give an outgrown toy to a friend, younger sibling, or charity. This cure not only keeps toy collections from expanding ad infinitum, it encourages kids to share with others.

Install pegboards or hooks in children's rooms.
Closet bars are often too high for young children to reach and can discourage neatness. Make it easy for kids to hang up their clothes by installing pegboards or hooks at a convenient height. If possible, lower clothing rods so they are more convenient.

Buy kid-sized hangers for children.
Standard hangers are too big for children's clothing. Buy kid-sized hangers that are scaled down to fit their clothes—and colorful plastic ones are more fun to use than conventional wire hangers.

Furnish children's rooms with easily accessible storage pieces.
Adult-size dressers and chests of drawers may be too tall for young children to access conveniently. Low-to-the-floor chests of drawers, trunks, and beds with integrated shelves or storage drawers underneath the mattress are easier for them to reach.

Let kids hold a mini–yard sale.
Kids can have fun and earn extra money by holding their own mini–yard sale. Encourage young entrepreneurs to sell toys they no longer play with. Cleaning their rooms becomes fun when they can turn their own clutter into cash.

Remove articles that symbolize conflict from the Helpful People Gua of a child's room.

The symbolism associated with war-oriented video games, toy soldiers, action hero dolls, play guns, etc., can have a destructive effect on a child's relationships with other kids. If your child plays with toys that have potentially violent associations, move these from the Helpful People Gua, which relates to friendship. This cure discourages conflict and encourages cooperation and congeniality between children—it can also help a child make new friends.

Give children their own clothes hampers.
Brightly colored plastic bins or cloth hampers in whimsical shapes designed to hang on the back of a closet door can inspire kids to pick up their dirty clothes. When they change clothes, they can immediately toss dirty ones into their very own laundry baskets. This can also make it easier for you to organize dirty laundry on wash day.

Simplify bed making for kids.
Buy bedding that makes it quick and easy for kids to make their own beds—comforters, for instance, are more convenient for children to use than several layers of sheets, blankets, and bedspreads. If you let kids choose their own colorful, whimsical, or hobby-oriented bedding, they'll be more likely to make their beds.

Give each child towels of a different color.
Cut down on laundry by assigning each child a towel color of his or her own choosing. Give each child two towels in his or her special color. Then make them responsible for keeping track of their towels, hanging them up, and putting them in the laundry basket.

Arrange three items that signify positive goals in the Future Gua of a child's room.
Three is the number of growth and putting ideas into action. Choose three objects that symbolize positive goals and accomplishment—sports trophies, blue ribbons, diplomas, a telescope, painting supplies, or a chemistry set, for example. Display these neatly in the Future Gua of the child's room to encourage success and achievement.

Allow each child one idiosyncratic collection they never have to prune.

While encouraging children to be neat and orderly by reducing clutter in other areas of their lives, allow them to have one special collection that they never have to prune. For one child, this might be a collection of stuffed animals; another might collect rocks or baseball cards or toy cars. Stipulate that they must keep their collections organized and contained within their own rooms (or another designated spot), rather than allowing these to overflow into the rest of the home.

Let kids choose household chores.

Like adults, kids may prefer to do some household chores rather than others. If there are several children in the family, allow them to work out with their siblings who will do what, so that everyone assumes his or her fair share.

Rotate children's chores.
Allowing children to rotate their chores on a weekly basis encourages them to master a variety of tasks while also reducing the boredom factor.

Give children their own workstations.
To help kids keep their schoolwork in order and encourage learning, provide each child with his or her own desk, chair, lamp, and bookcase. If possible, place these in the Knowledge Gua of the child's room (or the room where he or she does homework).

Improve a child's dusting skill.
To make sure a child dusts all those nooks and crannies, hide loose change in often-missed spots. The more effective the duster is, the more money he or she will make.

Corral bath toys in a basket beside the tub.
Rather than allowing toys to remain in the tub—or on the floor—after bath time, corral them neatly in a basket or colorful plastic bin beside the tub.

Nab toys left lying around the house or yard.
If kids neglect to pick up toys and put them away after playing with them, collect errant toys and hold them for ransom. Children can reclaim their toys by doing extra chores or other good deeds.

Strengthen a child's sense of self.
Arrange nine items that a child particularly likes and that represent positive goals or ideals in the Self/Identity Gua of his or her room.

~

Limit TV time.
Often, television and video games become "babysitters" for kids. But devoting too much time to these activities can interfere with a child's creative development. Studies also show that obesity is increasing among today's kids because they are too sedentary. Limit the amount of time kids spend watching TV and encourage them to pursue other interests and activities instead.

Curb a child's hyperactivity.

Objects that represent the fire element stimulate activity, individuality, and vitality. But too much of this element can cause hyperactivity and stress. Reduce the number of fire items—TV, computer, red- or orange-colored objects, action toys—in a child's room to tone down the tension surrounding him or her.

TIP: Articles that embody the earth and metal elements can help offset fire's influence and promote stability—see Chapter Three for more information.

Limit children's activities.
Many children are involved in so many activities—sports, music lessons, dance classes, etc.—that they have little down-time. Overbooking a child's schedule can clutter their lives and yours, creating stress for everyone. Determine which activities are most important and eliminate the others.

Give away unclaimed toys.
If a child doesn't miss a toy you've confiscated after a period of time, give it away. He or she probably doesn't need it.

CHAPTER EIGHT

Control Clutter in Your Personal Life

Do one thing at a time.
Instead of multitasking, focus on one task at a time and devote yourself to it completely. When you try to do several things at once, you can't pay attention to—or enjoy—any of them fully. Confusion, stress, and forgetfulness are the likely results.

Meditate regularly.
Many spiritual and healing traditions recommend daily meditation as a way to clear the mind and balance emotions. Just ten minutes a day can reduce stress, help center your mind, and increase your sense of well-being. Professional athletes have even discovered that meditation can improve their skills. Set aside a brief period every day (preferably the same time each day) to meditate or to simply sit quietly—think of this as your personal uncluttering time.

Read inspirational literature.
Begin each day by reading something inspirational—the *I Ching*, Rumi's poetry, or a religious text, for instance. This morning ritual helps to clear the mind of negativity and provides nourishing food for thought throughout the day.

Establish a personal centering ritual.
We all engage in rituals, from simple routine activities such as a morning coffee break to observing holiday traditions. Rituals serve as guideposts and centering devices that help us establish a sense of order in our lives. Create a daily personal centering ritual to calm the mind and balance emotions; for example, burn incense, go for a walk, or take a relaxing bath before bed.

Ring a bell to focus your mind.
Ring a bell or chime whenever you begin to feel scattered, stressed, or tired. The pleasing sound will focus your mind and bring you back to the present. Ringing bells and chimes also breaks up and disperses atmospheric clutter that can produce tension in your environment.

Think positive thoughts while you cook.
Your intention is the most important part of feng shui. Your thoughts and feelings are absorbed by the food you prepare, so when you eat it you take those thoughts and emotions into your body. You can actually "feed" yourself nourishing thoughts if you focus on upbeat, positive images while cooking.

Ring a dinner gong before eating.
In China, gongs are sometimes rung before meals to chase away unwanted energies and clear psychological clutter so those dining can eat in peace and harmony. The sound of a gong also serves as a trigger to stimulate the appetite, as the experiments of scientific researcher Ivan Petrovich Pavlov demonstrated, and improve digestion.

Make lists.

It's difficult and stressful to try to remember all the things you need to do. Keep lots of lists, so you don't forget something important. Neatly organize them in a notebook or loose-leaf binder that lets you remove or add pages as needed. Crossing off completed tasks adds to your sense of accomplishment.

Prioritize daily tasks.

Rank the items on your to-do list according to their importance or urgency. Take care of the first three—or more, if possible—so that at the end of the day you'll know you've accomplished something.

Organize your schedule to suit your own rhythms.

Some of us are morning people, others are night people. We all have our own circadian rhythms and tend to function more effectively when we pay attention to them. Organize your schedule to coincide with your own cycles. Try to undertake challenging tasks or those that require you to be mentally sharp during your peak-performance periods. Save less demanding ones for downtimes.

> TIP: Pay attention to your biorhythms, too. These operate on a more or less monthly basis—half of the time you are in an upswing period, the other half you are on the downswing. Track these and try to plan your activities accordingly.

Keep a notepad beside your bed.
Many people wake up in the middle of the night thinking about all the things they have to do the next day. Rather than trying to remember everything, which may interfere with your sleep, jot them down on a handy notepad. You may want to note your dreams here, too, so you don't forget them in the morning—dreams offer guidance and advice for solving problems during our waking hours.

Keep a journal.
Rather than running thoughts and impressions through your mind, record them in a journal. This reduces mental clutter and sparks further insights. Keeping a journal is a good way to log your personal growth experiences and work through problems, too.

Carry on one conversation at a time.

"Conversation clutter" occurs when we try to talk to several people at a time, interrupting each other and jumping from one conversation to another. This prevents us from giving our full attention to anyone and may cause confusion or misunderstanding. It can also show a lack of respect for the speaker. Conducting a single conversation that involves all the members of a group encourages togetherness and enables you to discuss a subject with greater depth and clarity.

Don't watch TV while eating.

The television set is a regular guest at many dinner tables. Instead of watching the six o'clock news while you eat, focus on your dining companions to improve relationships with family members and friends. Watching TV clutters your mind with thoughts that can interfere with good digestion.

Turn off the TV.
Television has become an omnipresent force in our homes and even some workplaces, bombarding us with images and noise. Instead of allowing your mind to be cluttered with advertising slogans, violent scenes, and inane chatter, turn off the TV unless you really want to view something you consider worthwhile. Limit your viewing time and don't leave the TV on as background noise, where it will still influence you at a subconscious level.

Use automatic billing.
Many companies offer automatic billing, which can be convenient for some people—especially those who travel frequently. Authorizing creditors to take money directly from your account eliminates the need to write checks and prevents you from forgetting to pay a bill on time.

Pay bills as soon as they arrive.
Bills that languish unpaid are nagging reminders of debt and lack. Pay them promptly so they don't dam the flow of prosperity. You'll also avoid late charges and interest.

> TIP: Some people may find it easier to pay bills on a certain date. Contact credit card companies, utilities, insurance firms, and others to arrange convenient payment schedules.

File bills according to due date.
When bills arrive, file them according to the dates when they are due if you don't intend to pay them right away. This prioritizes debts and keeps you from accidentally missing a payment date.

Balance your checkbook.
An unbalanced checkbook suggests the existence of problems with handling money matters. By keeping your checkbook current, you show a willingness to take charge of your finances and, on a psychological level, you encourage prosperity. You might even discover an error in your favor!

Burn incense to reduce stress.
Burn incense to remove disruptive ambient energies and bad vibes that can disturb your emotional or mental harmony. Incense burning can also be a valuable adjunct to meditation and other rituals. According to aromatherapy principles, calming scents such as lavender, vanilla, and sweet orange trigger the limbic system in the brain and can actually reduce mental clutter and encourage serenity.

Burn incense to enhance clarity and memory.

Burn mint- or citrus-scented incense to cleanse your mind of mental clutter. As aromatherapy has shown, these invigorating fragrances enable you to think more clearly and remember more of what you read or hear.

Don't entertain negative thoughts.

Focusing on negative thoughts can make you feel discouraged, tense, or powerless. Dwelling on un-pleasant things may also magnify their significance in your life or give them more importance than they deserve. When negative thoughts pop into your head—especially ones concerning things you can't do anything about—push them aside and turn your attention to more positive matters.

Clear your Health Gua to promote well-being.

The center of your home is connected with your health. Clutter or obstacles in this area can lead to physical problems or exacerbate existing conditions. Broken or damaged objects in your Health Gua may symbolize physical impairments—fix them or get rid of them. Keep this area clean and in good repair to promote overall well-being.

TIP: Place something in your Health Gua that symbolizes vitality to you, such as a live plant.

Avoid constructing "what if" scenarios.
Stop cluttering your mind with all sorts of fantasy scenarios that could, perhaps, occur in the future—none of these may ever actually come to pass. Weaving endless "what if" possibilities is both tiring and unproductive. Reel in those restless thoughts, discipline your mind, and focus on the present instead. Most of all, stop worrying about things you can't do anything about anyway and turn your attention to handling the ones you can.

Organize paper money by denomination.
Arranging bills by denomination in your wallet makes it easy to see how much cash you have. It also lets you pull out the right bill and can prevent mistakes.

Clean out your pocketbook or wallet.
Remove clutter from your purse and/or wallet to make room for new money to come your way. Get rid of expired coupons, keys you don't use, old cosmetics—everything you no longer need. Put loose change in your money jar.

Reduce credit card clutter.
Do you have credit cards you rarely use? The more credit cards you have, the greater are your chances of losing a card, having one stolen, or becoming the victim of credit card fraud. Even if you don't use some of your cards, they still impact your credit rating, which may be lowered by having too many credit cards, regardless of whether you show outstanding balances on them. Cancel and cut up credit cards you don't use.

Fight fair.

Arguments with people close to you are probably inevitable, but you can minimize the amount of hurt or anger generated in a heated discussion if you fight fair. Don't intentionally say things to insult, demean, or wound someone else. Try not to let an argument escalate out of control by fanning the flames. Strive for win–win solutions, rather than attempting to get the better of another person.

Stick to the issues in an argument.

Often, we bring extraneous issues or old grievances into an argument. Instead of resolving matters, this can clutter a discussion and distract you from the main points. Stick to your primary concern and don't let yourself or others get sidetracked.

Delegate responsibilities to others.
Don't try to do everything yourself, even if you think you can handle tasks better than anyone else. Allow family members— especially children—to share the chores and responsibilities. This encourages them to feel more mature by taking on a larger role in the operation of the household. It can also reduce the clutter of duties and obligations in your daily life.

Don't drive kids everywhere they want to go.
Obesity is increasing among children because they don't get enough exercise. Whenever possible, encourage them to walk or ride bicycles to school, activities, and friends' homes. When that isn't feasible, carpool. Get them to plan ahead and coordinate their schedules so you don't clutter up your day making numerous trips, or let them take public transportation to gain a sense of independence.

Read romantic poetry to improve your love life.
Before going to sleep, read a romantic poem. This cure helps to reduce mental clutter and focuses your mind on the goal of improving your love life. Sweet dreams!

Write a letter to someone you've been meaning to contact.
Receiving a letter from someone you haven't heard from in a while can brighten your day. Make someone else's day by writing a letter or sending an e-mail. From the perspective of feng shui, putting things off delays good fortune and can interfere with your sense of accomplishment. This cure helps to unclutter your mind by removing an item from your to-do list.

Set aside family togetherness time.

We tend to involve ourselves in so many outside activities that we may overlook the importance of spending time with loved ones and family members. Schedule time for family togetherness, just as you would book any other type of appointment. Shared family time should involve all members and engage everyone in positive personal interactions—watching TV and similar passive diversions don't count. Take turns deciding what you will do together as a family.

Make a will.

None of us wants to think we're going to die, but the reality is that we all will. Make it easy for your loved ones to disperse your treasures—and get rid of any clutter you leave behind—by clearly specifying who gets what and how your affairs are to be handled after your passing. A will can help relieve confusion, guilt, and stress during a time when grief may add to the difficulty of making important decisions.

~

Assess your expectations of others.
Take a good, hard look at what you expect of other people and why. Are your expectations fair and realistic? Who are they intended to benefit? What point or result do you expect as an outcome? Sometimes so-called good intentions may be misdirected, such as when you encourage a child to take music lessons because you always wanted to play the piano or pressure a partner to climb the corporate ladder because you desire status. Some expectations may be reasonable and warranted, others may create emotional clutter for the people we care about.

Assess other people's expectations of you.
Are other people cluttering your life with their expectations? Do relatives expect you to spend every holiday with them? Does a partner expect you to handle most of the child care? Do friends drop by unannounced and expect you to entertain them? Determine which expectations are producing tension or burdening you, then work on finding constructive ways to limit unreasonable demands.

Unclutter your diet.
Most of us could benefit from a little dietary uncluttering. Eliminate junk food and clean up your diet—you'll feel better and look better, too. You'll also save money.

Learn to say no.

Most of us accept invitations to events we'd rather not attend and agree to assume duties we don't want responsibility for. Instead of cluttering up your schedule with activities you find unpleasant, unrewarding, or unnecessary, learn to decline politely—without feeling guilty.

Use ribbons as reminders.

Tie ribbons in prominent places—on the kitchen faucet, your car steering wheel, your telephone receiver—to help you remember things you need to do. You may want to color-code the ribbons to provide additional information—a green ribbon on your phone might prompt you to make a doctor's appointment; a red ribbon tied around your bedpost could remind you to buy a birthday present for a significant other.

Select your companions carefully.
Other people can take up a lot of time and emotional
energy. They may even clutter your life with their problems,
needs, and demands. Be selective about the people with whom
you associate—weed out the ones who drain your energy, who
aren't good for you, or whose company you don't particularly
like. You'll have more time to enjoy the special people in your
life or to do things by yourself.

Don't put things off.
If possible, address tasks right away rather than putting them
off until some unspecified time in the future. Postponing a task
not only increases the number of things you'll have to deal with
later, it also produces nagging feelings of inadequacy and
incompetence. Knowing a chore is looming ahead can drain
your vitality and cast a shadow over your day.

Take time out.

Give yourself a break each day to unclutter your mind and emotions. Do something you really enjoy—by yourself, for yourself—even if it's only for a few minutes. Take a hot bath, listen to relaxing music, go for a walk—whatever soothes your body and soul.

Resources

Alexander, Skye. *10-Minute Feng Shui*. Gloucester, MA: Fair Winds Press/Rockport Publishers, 2002.

Hemphill, Barbara. *Taming the Paper Tiger*. 4th ed. Washington, D.C.: Kiplinger, 1997.

Kingston, Karen. *Clear Your Clutter with Feng Shui*. New York: Broadway Books, 1999.

Rechtschaffen, Stephan. *Timeshifting: Creating More Time to Enjoy Your Life*. New York: Doubleday, 1996.

Skolnik, Lisa. *The Right Storage: Organizing Essentials for the Home*. Gloucester, MA: Rockport Publishers, 2001.

About the Author

Skye Alexander is the author of *10-Minute Feng Shui, 10-Minute Crystal Ball, 10-Minute Magic Spells, 10-Minute Tarot, Magickal Astrology, Planets in Signs,* and the mystery novel *Hidden Agenda.* A contributing author to *Your Birthday Sign Through Time, Love Signs and You, A Taste of Murder, Undertow, Mystery in Mind,* and *AstroMysteries,* she has also written for numerous magazines, newspapers, TV, and radio. She lives in Massachusetts with her cat, Domino.